The SEXY BOOK of SEXY SEX

BY KRISTEN SCHAAL AND RICH BLOMQUIST

Illustrations by Michael Kupperman and Lisa Hanawalt

CHRONICLE BOOKS

SAN FRANCISCO

Text copyright © 2010 by Kristen Schaal and Rich Blomquist.
Cover and Author Photographs © 2010 by Gretchen LeMaistre

Chronicle Books would like to thank Emily Craig, Jenny Traig, Carey
Jones, Kim Romero, Ben Kasman, Sandy Lynn Davis, Amanda Moyrong,
Julie Romeis, Lindsay Sablosky, Jenna Cushner, Oscar Stowell, Gretchen
LeMaistre, Kirk Crippens, Lisa Hanawalt, Michael Kupperman, Tim
Belonax, Rachel Weill, Daniel Greenberg, Beth Steiner, Dean Burrell,
Becca Cohen, Lynda Carter, Loni Anderson, and Rihanna for their
contributions to this book.

COVER IMAGE:

Photography and Illustration: Gretchen LeMaistre
Makeup artist: Christina Schock
The photographer would like to thank James Hickey.

ILLUSTRATION CREDITS:

Chapter opener illustrations, p. 12, 22, 46, 62, 80, 106, 122, 148, 170;
Wildo's Retreat, p. 132-133: © Lisa Hanawalt

Illustrations, p. 21, 27, 28, 30-31, 32, 69, 70-71, 94-95, 109-110, 134-135,
140-141, 154, 155, 156, 164-165, 167-169, 174, 176-177, 179: © Michael
Kupperman

Augmentooming, p. 50: © Oguz Aral

Library of Congress Cataloging-in-Publication Data available.
ISBN 978-0-8118-7126-6

Manufactured in the United States.
Designed by Michael Morris and Emily Craig, p.i.c.

10 9 8 7 6 5 4 3 2 1

Chronicle Books LLC
680 Second Street
San Francisco, California 94107
www.chroniclebooks.com

Contents

A Word from the Authors

Sex is the most powerful and important thing in the universe, and if you're not instantly good at it, you probably never will be and everyone will laugh at you.

This is something you should know before even *attempting* sex.

Fortunately, you are holding **The Ultimate Guide to Sex: Unabridged, Un-Spell-Checked, and Uncircumsized**, completed in the Year of Our Loins Two Thousand and Ten by Ms. Kristen Schaal and Mr. Rich Blomquist and subsequently redubbed *The Sexy Book of Sexy Sex* because the aforementioned title had already been taken. So, relax. You're in good hands.

But BEWARE!!! This sexy knowledge comes with a terrible price:

First, a suggested retail of $24.95 ($29.95 in Canada). Admittedly on the high end for this type of book, but the authors have to eat.

Second—and far more important—*after you have read this book, there is **no going back***.

Once absorbed, the lessons contained in *The Sexy Book of Sexy Sex* cannot be unlearned. Armed with the bawdy wisdom on any given page, you could easily spend the rest of your life orgasming your brains out, neglecting your friendships, your career, and every other aspect of your life that doesn't involve constant genital stimulation. To call you a "mindless sex zombie" would be putting it gently. And perhaps the scariest part: you would be *completely satisfied* . . . as would your legions of sexual partners.

WELL, ARE YOU IN?

If so, turn the page.[*]

[*]Note: In turning this page, You, hereafter referred to as "Reader," hereby absolve the Authors of any and all liability for consequences suffered as a result of the sexy lessons contained herein, including but not limited to sex zombism, either mindless or mindful.

How to Use This Book

This publication is intended to be a comprehensive guide to sex and all things sex-related, from courtship, to foreplay, to more foreplay, to just a little more foreplay, to actually banging. Great care and effort were taken to make this book as complete as possible. If you can think of a sex question not answered in this manual, it's only because federal, state, or local laws prohibit you from asking it. It is NOT because the authors don't know the answer, because *we do*.

That said, with a book this sexy there will be times you aren't interested in learning—*just in achieving orgasm as quickly and spectacularly as possible*. For that reason, the most erotic and titillating parts of this guide are printed in red.

Go ahead. Skip to the steamiest, most profane passages in this jizz-soaked wank rag that dares call itself a book. Feast your eyes and your imagination on forbidden words that were until now only whispered by drunken lovers and Japanese businessmen with Tourette's—words like splooge burglar, choad gobbler, and queef nugget. Are you blushing? If so, *stop*. The sooner you let go of your inhibitions, the sooner you can forgo embarrassment and get that extra face blood into your genitals where it belongs.

How *Not* to Use This Book

As you read, you will no doubt come to associate this guide with *pure erotic pleasure*. However, under NO CIRCUMSTANCES should you insert this book into ANY orifice for purposes of sexual gratification. It is bound with cheap Chinese glue that will POISON YOU.

Why We Are Qualified to Write This Book

Anyone can write a book. But not everyone can *live* a book.

Every sexual technique described in this manual *we have tried.* Every erogenous zone *we have erogenated.* Every STD *we have suffered from*—sometimes for way too long—just to see what would happen. A lot of blood, sweat, and foul-smelling yellow discharge went into the writing of this guide.

Why? Certainly not for profit. No amount of money could make up for the lovemaking sessions we sacrificed so we could slave away at our waterproof Jacuzzi computers. To put it mildly: IT WAS HELL! In fact, we had no intention of becoming authors at all until we came to a boner-chilling realization: THIS BOOK WOULD SAVE LIVES. In fact, it's already saved the life of someone very important to us . . . YOU. A few pages ago, the finely tuned sexual instrument that is YOU was dying of a serious disease, your pleasure-starved genitals wasting away from a lack of carnal sustenance. You didn't realize it at the time but you were very sick. To put it in medical terms, you were totally sexorexic.

So what qualifies us to write this book? That's a funny thing to ask someone who just saved your life.

Where to Hide This Book from Your Children

Refrigerator vegetable drawer

In church

Inside any other boring sex book

CHAPTER 1

Sex in Nature

The Origin of the Sexy

Humans did not invent sex.

Like burrowing, scampering, and throwing feces, man owes a debt of gratitude to **nature** for paving the way. It is because of sex that favorable genes are passed from one generation to the next, making it stronger, healthier, and all-around more fuckable.

But it was *homo and hetero sapiens* who elevated sex to staggering new heights. Armed with a superior intellect, a relentless desire for better orgasms, and opposable thumbs that could reach our own genitals, we single- and double-handedly transformed sex from merely surviving to really *living*. In fact, human copulation is widely recognized as the best sex in the universe. It is our greatest achievement and our legacy . . . and *we're only getting better at it.*

Still, man can learn a lot from animals: how to find an appropriate mate, how to complete the transfer of bodily fluids while looking out for predators, and most important, how to abandon said mate after obtaining sexual gratification with little to no awkwardness (even if it means biting their head off). In many ways, animals are nature's sex ed teachers minus the condom and the banana, unless you're watching baboons fuck in the zoo, in which case one of them might have a banana.

They say those who do not learn from history are doomed to repeat it. But one pays an even bigger price for not being a good student of nature. Because **those who fail to learn from animals will never fuck like one.**

The similarity to unicorns isn't the only reason girls love ponies.

Asexual Reproduction:
Too Good to Share

Before sex, life was a lot less complicated. So was making more of it. Single-cell organisms reproduced **asexually**, meaning "without humping." There were no STDs, no stalkers, no erectile dysfunctions, and no lame bachelor parties with strippers jumping out of cakes you were really excited to eat. At parties, cells would simply slip into the bathroom and divide, then sneak out hoping no one would notice there were two of them. And even if they did, *nobody cared*. What happened in the primordial ooze stayed in the primordial ooze.

Though convenient, asexual reproduction has its drawbacks, including:

- No fucking

- No sucking

- Limited variation from generation to generation, resulting in fewer genetic alternatives and decreased adaptability

- Did we mention no fucking or sucking?

By definition, asexual reproduction is not as sexy as sexual reproduction. But what it lacks in quality, it makes up for in quantity. Some types of bacteria can double their numbers every twenty minutes—that's like having repetitive, joyless sex seventy-two times a day! For this reason, biologists have dubbed bacteria "Nature's porn star."

Even as life on this planet became more complex and infinitely more doable, some shy species continued having sex with themselves, each subsequent generation risking blindness and/or hairy palms in the name of survival.

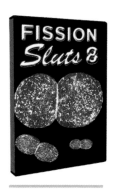

*For a genre with so many graphic close-ups, **asexual porn** does not come close to a turn-on.*

Creatures That Produce Asexually (and why they do it)				
			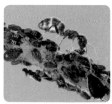

Hammerhead Sharks
Commitment issues

Komodo Dragons
Devout Catholics

Some Snails
Apartment too cramped to bring anyone back to

Aphids
Penises so small sex isn't worth the trouble

The Klama Sutra

The first treatise on sexual intercourse dates back to the Cambrian period, some five hundred million years ago. Discovered in present-day India, the Klama Sutra described dozens of sexual positions meant to enhance lovemvaking and spice up fizzling mollusk marriages.

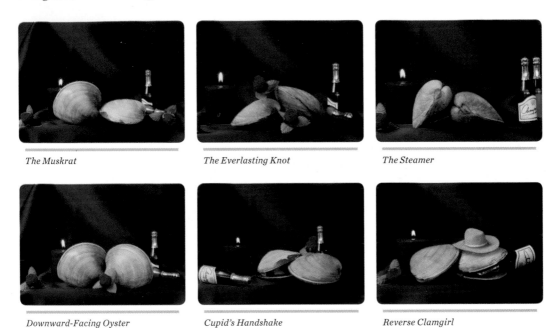

The Muskrat   *The Everlasting Knot*   *The Steamer*

Downward-Facing Oyster   *Cupid's Handshake*   *Reverse Clamgirl*

Animal Courtship: Booty Call of the Wild

Imagine trying to find your ideal companion in the untamed wilderness, or in the depths of the deepest ocean. Hundreds of miles may stand between you and your soul mate, or maybe you scuttle past each other every day and never realize it, two desperate, anonymous souls in a colony of millions. How would you find each other?

You probably wouldn't.

Fortunately, most animals are just looking for something to boink, not to love. But simply being noticed is no easy task in the sweaty, twenty-four-hour discothèque we call Nature. For that reason, some sexy species have raised their game, performing unique courtship rituals that make it virtually impossible to ignore their junk.

Great Pickup Artists of the Animal Kingdom

SPECIES	COURTSHIP BEHAVIOR	HUMAN EQUIVALENT
	Look at me! Look at me! Part of me lights up! Isn't that incredible? Oh shit. I just realized there are a thousand other douche bags here doing the exact same thing.	
	Males have 400 distinct calls to attract a mate.	
	Exhaust themselves swimming hundreds of miles in hopes of a single pity fuck.	
	Dominant males have "harems" of 30 to 100 cows. To increase chances of mating, females are not allowed to drive.	
	Squid couples begin having sex at sunrise and continue all day, only stopping at twilight to eat and rest.	
	Spend 9 or 10 months each year constructing a bower, a shelter they meticulously decorate with seashells, berries, leaves, and flowers in order to trick potential mates into thinking they are creative and nurturing.	

The Mud Shark:
Nature's Dildo

If tuna is the chicken of the sea, the vibrator of the sea is none other than the mud shark. Between its dorsal spines, slippery skin, and legendary patience, *Squalus acanthias* is perfectly suited for pleasuring a female human. But it was a young rock band by the name of Led Zeppelin that secured the mud shark's place in the pantheon of sexy animals.

The mud shark accounts for the high mercury content in early heavy metal.

The Legend

On July 28, 1969, Led Zeppelin and their road manager, Richard Cole, were staying at the Edgewater Inn following a performance at the Seattle Pop Festival. The hotel, located on a pier overlooking Puget Sound, encouraged guests to "fish from their rooms," presumably an attempt to compensate for the worst room service in the greater Seattle area. Avid fishermen, the bandmates cast a few lines out of their windows, and soon their luxury suite was knee-deep in salmon, cod, pollock, and an active WWII mine John Paul Jones had wrestled to the surface thinking it was a giant puffer fish.

Suddenly, there was a flirtatious knock on the door. Behind it stood a strikingly gorgeous Seattle-area groupie with red hair, attracted by the smell of halibut and British Sterling.

Exactly what happened next has been lost to history, but theories include:

- Finding themselves in a room full of marine life and a willing Zeppelinette, the band naturally took turns pleasuring her with different species of fish. But from the first moment John Bonham touched a mud shark to the groupie's snatch, it was obvious to everyone in the room that the slippery brown predator and female genitalia were meant to be together. In the span of half an hour, the groupie was rocked by dozens of the most satisfying, soul-shaking orgasms she had ever experienced. Word got out, and the mud shark quickly became popular with shut-ins and lesbian fisherwomen.

- The starstruck fan found herself at the center of a genuine rock 'n' roll orgy, but it was a far cry from the "stairway to heaven" she had long dreamed about. After twenty minutes, the band and their manager were deep in postcoital slumber, leaving it to the turned-on groupie to finish herself off. She grabbed a mud shark off the floor, and nine months later gave birth to a beautiful mermaid baby, who would go on to become the bassist for Slipknot.

- In a fit of ecstasy the groupie accidentally pulled off John Bonham's mask revealing he was a secret mud shark. The rest of the band pleaded with the girl not to tell anybody, especially given that good drummers were hard to come by. The groupie agreed, on the condition that she be allowed to tell the "Led Zeppelin fucked me with a mud shark" part of the story. The band had no problem with that rumor getting out, since it would boost their cred in both the rock 'n' roll and fishing communities.

Whatever happened, the mud shark's destiny was forever changed. Today, the unassuming fish is worth its weight in gold, and many mud sharks find themselves living a life of erotic luxury of which they never dreamed. If dog is man's best friend, then surely woman's is the mud shark.

Our Life with the Bonobos

Only one other creature rivals humans in horniness: the bonobo ape. And in that contest the bonobo takes the cake. Then it fucks the cake. Then it eats the cake while it fucks another bonobo, also eating the cake. Then several other bonobos join in, all of them eating and/or fucking cake.

While that may sound depraved even by monkey standards, the emphasis on sex in bonobo culture actually serves a sophisticated purpose: it defuses conflict. This is something we learned firsthand when we spent three months living among the bonobos, studying them, photographing them, and being sexually intimidated by them.

TODAY WE witnessed two MALE BONOBOS SETTLE a dispute OVER a MANGO BY "PENIS FENCING," A Ritual IN WHICH THE AGGRIEVED PARTIES HANG FROM a TREE LIMB aND PUB PENISES TOGETHER. IF WE CAN BRING THIS KNOWLEDGE BACK TO CIVILIZATION, WE MAY HAVE FOUND a SOLUTION TO MANKIND'S INABILITY TO MAKE a PORNO WITH a DECENT ACTION SEQUENCE.

THOUGH THE MALES ARE STRONGER, THE BONOBO SOCIETY IS DOMINATED BY THE FEMALES, WHO SOMETIMES "GANG UP" TO OVERPOWER LONE MALES, THE LESSON BEING: A PENIS SWORD IS NO MATCH AGAINST GOOD OLD-FASHIONED PUSSY WHIPS.

BONOBO LANGUAGE

"GOOD MORNING" = THREE GENITAL BUMPS aND a TONGUE KISS

"CAN I HAVE SOME SUGAR CANE?" = THIRTEEN SECONDS OF FACE HUMPING

"MOVE OVER" = ONE GENITAL RUB ON THE SHOULDER FOLLOWED BY PENETRATION

"THANK YOU" = GENEROUS ANAL FISTING

HUMAN SEXUAL BEHAVIORS PRACTICED BY BONOBOS

TONGUE KISSING

ORAL SEX

FACE-TO-FACE INTERCOURSE

UNIVERSITY LAB

EXPERIMENTATION IN COLLEGE

FUCKTOID

Before it went extinct, the **STD carrier pigeon** had a great time.

For a nonmigratory bird, the STD carrier pigeon really got around.

CHAPTER 2

The History of Sex

Cock of Ages

Even before she was whisked away to Troy, Helen was making oral history.

Sexual intercourse has not only produced the generations of humans responsible for making history, it's been the driving force behind it. The Trojan War? Fought over a sexy lady. The Church of England's schism with Roman Catholicism? Henry VIII's answer to a cock-blocking pope. The discovery of penicillin? The result of Alexander Fleming's unrelenting quest to cure his game-killing gonorrhea (both of which he stumbled upon by accident). Given the prevalence of sex throughout the course of civilization, it's a wonder the pages of history aren't stuck together.

We know what you're thinking: *I thought this was supposed to be a SEX book. Why are they wasting valuable pages talking about a bunch of dead people?* Well, two reasons. First, as people who lived through the Black Death learned, the dead can be very sexy, especially when all the living ones are terrified of human contact. And second, even though sex has only gotten better with time, we still have much to learn from the past. To put it another way: *you don't know where penises are going until you know where penises have been.* So, where *have* they been? The answer, much like an unexpectedly placed penis, may surprise you.

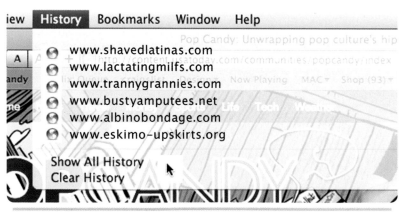

When it comes to sexual histories, it doesn't get more revealing than your roommate's browser history

Adam and Eve:
Testing Out the Equipment

Adam and Eve were created in God's image with one unmistakable difference: genitals. God doesn't have a penis or a vagina because frankly, He doesn't need One. He exists in a state of constant orgasm infinitely more enjoyable than anything mere mortals can hope to experience (unless they've read this book). So when the Creator scooped a hole in Eve's crotch, rolled the leftover material between His palms, and stuck the resulting fleshy cigar thing under Adam's washboard abs, it was something of an experiment. Fortunately, He couldn't have picked two better scientists.

Contrary to rumors you hear in the church locker room, Adam and Eve did *not* get kicked out of the Garden of Eden because they had premarital sex. If anything, God encouraged them to make love, telling them to "be fruitful and multiply." What got Adam and Eve two one-way tickets to Mortality Town was the fact that they got freaky. *Really* freaky.

Though easily concealed with a single leaf, Adam took comfort knowing his package was still bigger than God's.

First they did it in the communal watering hole. Then they did it on the back of a dinosaur. Then they crafted a sex swing out of some vines and made the dinosaur watch. God could hardly believe His all-seeing eyes. He had created genitals for fitting nicely together, not for all this kinky shit (He may have even been a little jealous, not having a Mrs. God to fool around with). The final straw came when Eve fashioned a ball gag for Adam out of an apple God had specifically told them not to touch. Eve tried to tell Him she was just "being fruitful," but He was in no mood for wordplay. Adam and Eve had gone too far.

Clothes Encounters of the First Kind
Leaves weren't the first things Adam and Eve grabbed to cover their all-of-a-sudden naughty bits.

Serpents   *Bagels*   *Handwritten apologies*

God cast His sexual guinea pigs out of the Garden. Even worse, He made them aware of their nakedness, and Adam and Eve shamefully covered the tingly bits they had once so proudly flaunted in front of the triceratopses. It would take thousands of years of sexual repression and guilty masturbating in the dark for intercourse to stop feeling "dirty." Yet despite their crime against the Dickless Wonder upstairs and the eternal punishment it brought, Adam and Eve had scored a major victory for humankind: they had figured out that the wang-doodle goes in the hoo-ha.

Fertility Statues

Throughout history, some of mankind's favorite objects have been sex objects. Here are some of the most notable, ranked according to sexiness:

Venus of Willendorf
FERTILITY: 8.5

The stereotype-defying Phallus of Kyoto
FERTILITY: 9.2

Das Eisenwomb (The Iron Uterus)
FERTILITY: 2.5

Twelve-Boobed Cock of Katmandu
FERTILITY: 10.0

ᴀ Brief History of Sex

PREHISTORIC ERA

200,000 BC: Men and women awkwardly congregate on opposite sides of Pangaea, waiting for someone to make the first move.

200,000 and one hour later BC: Men and women attempt sex for the first time. Women's vaginas instinctively evolve hymens.

JESUS TIMES

0: Virgin birth sparks fears of getting pregnant from toilet seats.

33: Masturbation falls to all-time low given possibility of Jesus actually watching.

ANCIENT HISTORY

3500 BC: Enterprising women found world's first profession.

1100 BC: In Greece, nude wrestling plus copious amounts of olive oil inevitably leads to sodomy.

INDUSTRIAL REVOLUTION

1801: Rampant child labor gives parents some alone time, especially after death of child.

1908: Assembly line's emphasis on fitting pieces together as fast as possible leads to invention of the quickie.

DARK AGES

1355: Necrophilia invented; dating scene flourishes.

RENAISSANCE

1474: Lorenzo de Medici becomes first and last man to get laid at a Renaissance fair.

GREAT DEPRESSION

1930: Tough economic times turn vaginas into dust bowls.

1485: Secretly gay Leonardo da Vinci envisions ways to trap men in giant circles.

1934: Bonnie and Clyde make love in vault, accidentally inventing the sperm bank.

WORLD WAR II

1942: Rosie the Riveter encourages women to help war effort by becoming lesbians.

1945: After witnessing horrors of war, sexual harassment no big deal.

THE 1980S (AKA THE AIDSTIES)

1981: Snorting cocaine off boners invented.

1987: Victims of AIDS honored with quilt impossible to decorate a room around.

SEXUAL REVOLUTION

1960: Birth control becomes first form of control granted to women.

1961: Term "slut" coined for women exercising their control.

THE GOLDEN AGE OF SEX

1998: As a favor to women everywhere, Viagra instantly covered by insurance companies (birth control not so much).

2008: Having exhausted all other sexual fetishes, people decide vampires are sexy.

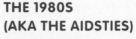

A Series of Tubes:
Female Anatomy through History

In olden times women were forbidden from exploring their bodies. Those hands were better used for making sandwiches, giving hand jobs, or if the woman was especially talented, doing both at the same time. Uncharted and untamed, the feminine wilderness became the stuff of legend, leading to wild speculation about what exactly was up there.

BIBLICAL

(6000 B.C. – A.D. 1000)

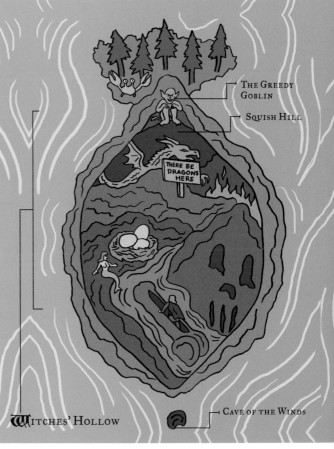

"LOWER EARTH"

(1000 – 1959)

FREE LOVE HOLE
(SEXUAL RFVOLUTION 1960 – 1975)

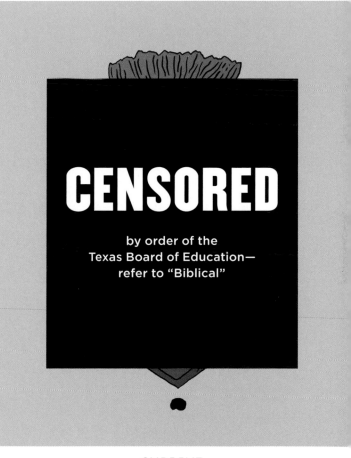

CENSORED

by order of the
Texas Board of Education—
refer to "Biblical"

CURRENT

The Day the Earth Didn't Stand Still:
Discovery of the Female Orgasm

Ra bless you.

Unlike its male equivalent, the female orgasm is a complicated and unwieldy process involving candles, smooth jazz, rose petals, terrycloth robes, and just the right amount of peppermint schnapps. Scholars initially believed that Cleopatra—with her throngs of male attendants and loose-fitting garments—was the first woman to achieve orgasm. This was disproved, however, when analysis of a hieroglyph depicting the event concluded she had only sneezed.

Scientists now believe the first female orgasm was experienced in 1897 by Flora Stanley, wife of American inventor Freelan O. Stanley. Mr. Stanley is best remembered for his steam-powered automobile, but it is Flora who really got engines started.

We were allowed to publish the following entries from her very private journal.

Dear Diary,

Today Freelan woke me up before dawn because he wanted to "make love." At least that's what Freelan calls it. I call it dry well paddling. For a man who helped finesse the piston, it's incredible how clumsy his penis is. It would make more sense if he invented the wet noodle. Honestly, the things I have to do to pass the time before it's over! I mostly just try to think about my favorite things, like cranberry sauce, the color blue, and Jesus. Sometimes I'll put them all together and Jesus and I are having a cranberry casserole in a blue castle. Before we get to the cranberry ice cream dessert Freelan is usually rolling off me and skipping off to the lab. He always has a spring in his step afterwards. I envy him. I feel heavy and drippy, and starving for cranberry sauce! Which we never have.

Dear Diary,

Sorry if my handwriting is indecipherable, I'm still shaking. Something very unusual happened to me today. I was dusting in Freelan's laboratory, like I always do on Tuesdays, and I noticed that he left the prototype for his new steam engine on. It was steaming away, piping warm air through this long cylindrical valve on the top. I went over to see if I could turn it off, but I don't think Freelan finished inventing the OFF switch.

I just ignored it and I climbed on top of the counter because I needed to dust off some test tubes and tongs and such, when I felt some of the steam push its way up my skirt and petticoats. It startled me! I knocked a couple of tubes to the floor. But the steam didn't care. It just kept pulsing warm moist air up to my secret place. It felt so good, my legs got weak. I swear I didn't have the strength to keep standing, that's why I had to sit down on the engine and my secret place just happened to be right up against the opening of the valve. Well, I didn't want my knickers to get wet, so I pushed them down to my knees and then all of a sudden the hot steam was shooting right up into my Netherlands! And I was paralyzed there. I promise I was suffering some form of a stroke because no matter how hard my brain told my body to move it just wouldn't! So there I was stuck on this steam engine as if I had become one of Freelan's experiments. And here's the thing, Diary, please do not tell ANYONE, but I started feeling this sensation that I have never felt before in my life. It's hard to describe, but it was as if Jesus had crawled inside of me with the steam and was polishing me with pleasure prayers. At least that's what I hope it was! It had to be, it was out of this world! And then the prayers got louder and turned into a chorus, it was like Jesus was performing an earthshaking sing-along, and my secret place was singing right back at him! And then I started to sing too, but it was less like singing and more like screaming, and Jesus just exploded inside of me and it was amazing! It felt like pleasure and pain and steam all rolled into one.

Luckily the steam ran out at that point and I was able to overcome my mild stroke and get off the engine. I picked up the test tube pieces and tried to act normal when Freelan came home for dinner. But I could barely contain my excitement at the fact that I had Jesus in my heart and my secret place!

Dear Diary,

Sorry again for the horrifying penmanship. I'm writing this to you in complete darkness. I am here at the Francis Dildo Sanitarium. I was sent here after Freelan caught me sitting on his steam engine again. I have gotten a bit reckless with how often I need to dust Freelan's lab, and my uniting with the steam engine seems to keep happening. When Freelan caught me saddling his engine and shaking with joy I tried to tell him Jesus was inside of me. But I suppose Freelan got a bit jealous of Jesus, which is understandable. Anyways, he checked me into the expensive Francis Dildo Sanitarium, and it's lights-out so I could be scribbling on the sheets for all I know, it's pitch-black!

But it's important that I get this down. I discovered that someone else checked into the Francis Dildo Sanitarium with me: Jesus! And thank goodness. To keep the residents' minds occupied we have afternoon projects every day. Mine has been candle making. I have been really trying to excel at my project, to demonstrate that I am well enough to return to my Freelan. But one afternoon I was dipping my candle and my mind started to wander, and when I looked down I had over-dipped the candle and it was thicker than usual. I didn't want them to see that I had made a mistake so I decided to hide the candle somewhere. The only place that I knew would be secret was my secret place. I slid it up there, and lo and behold Jesus was back! I slid it out and back again just to make sure, and couldn't help but let out a thankful amen. I have been so lonely here. But before I had a chance to really enjoy my time with Jesus, I looked up and saw Dr. Francis Dildo standing right there, watching me. He confiscated my candle and assigned me to pillow stuffing.

Francis Dildo patented the thick waxy candle and named it after himself. He made millions of dollars and never gave Flora any credit, or even a discount on her sanitarium bill. But as the old saying goes: it takes a Dildo to know a dildo.

FUCKTOID

Historians believe the heart symbol (♥) associated with love was inspired by the seed of the Silphium plant. Though now extinct, Silphium was used in ancient times as a form of birth control, along with clubs (♣), spades (♠), and holding out for a diamond (♦).

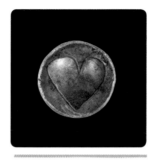

*An **ancient coin** glorifying birth control, used to this day as secret currency among liberals*

Cock 'n' Hole Hall of Fame

The closest most people will come to achieving a sexual legacy is producing a child, which, unfortunately, isn't all that impressive. But throughout history, a bulging handful of great lovers proved so skilled in the art of fleshly delights they became legend.

CASANOVA

SIGNATURE PICKUP MOVE:
Offered troubled women a shoulder to cry on, then subtly replaced shoulder with his penis.

CRAZIEST HOOKUP:
Unknowingly slept with his teenage daughter. Then, realizing what he'd done, knowingly slept with her.

ENDURING LEGACY:
The name "Casanova" became a catchall term for one who plays on women's emotions for sex, replacing earlier term "man."

CLEOPATRA

SIGNATURE PICKUP MOVE:
Sending a slave with tattoo "Do you like me? Check one: Yes __ No__" and a dull knife.

CRAZIEST HOOKUP:
Tossing Caesar's salad.

ENDURING LEGACY:
With a powerful kingdom at your command and a little eye makeup, you can get any man.

MARQUIS DE SADE

SIGNATURE PICKUP MOVE:
"You know the word sadism? That's named after me."

CRAZIEST HOOKUP:
Accidentally poisoned four prostitutes with Spanish fly-laced candy.

ENDURING LEGACY:
Invented green M&Ms.

CATHERINE THE GREAT

EMILY DICKINSON

LIBERACE

SIGNATURE PICKUP MOVE:
Presenting handful of
sugar cubes.

CRAZIEST HOOKUP:
A horse.

ENDURING LEGACY:
Gave birth to Paul I of Russia,
first in a long line of centaur
czars.

SIGNATURE PICKUP MOVE:
Staring coldly out window
at falling leaves of autumn,
reflecting on own mortality.

CRAZIEST HOOKUP:
Thomas Wentworth Higginson,
her "pen pal with benefits."

ENDURING LEGACY:
First cute goth chick.

SIGNATURE PICKUP MOVE:
Flamboyant fingering.

CRAZIEST HOOKUP:
Regrettable one-night stand
with a rusty candlestick and a
Moog.

ENDURING LEGACY:
Never came out of the closet,
which would have been moot
considering it was filled with
rhinestone capes and white
llama fur coats.

| WILT CHAMBERLAIN | MADONNA | HUGH HEFNER |

SIGNATURE PICKUP MOVE:
"I've had sex with twenty thousand women, but only because I was looking for you."

CRAZIEST HOOKUP:
The one night he decided to stay in and watch *Fried Green Tomatoes*, yet somehow still ended up banging eighteen women.

ENDURING LEGACY:
Proved being named "Wilt" doesn't necessarily mean you're impotent.

SIGNATURE PICKUP MOVE:
Being Madonna.

CRAZIEST HOOKUP:
Doing it with the devil in exchange for immortality.

ENDURING LEGACY:
Came up with something even more delicious than ice cream to put inside cones.

SIGNATURE PICKUP MOVE:
Playing his ribs like a xylophone.

CRAZIEST HOOKUP:
All of them.

ENDURING LEGACY:
Put the "man" in "creepy old mansion."

One of the biggest
misconceptions involving
religion and sex is that Orthodox
Jews only have sex through a hole in a
sheet. This is a stereotype rooted in ignorance and is an insult to the Jewish faith. The
only thing Jews cut a hole in is their foreskins,
with a jagged shard from a stomped-on wine glass
during a full moon. This ancient ritual endows
what's left of their penises with magical powers
and is the source of Jews' legendary sexual
prowess. Your only hope of experiencing
this kosher bliss is to trick a Jew into
making love to you. That's where
the sheet comes in . . .

ℳEDIEVAL ℳUNCHING

Int. King Henry's private chambers—night

KING HENRY and ANNE BOLEYN face each other on the royal bed amidst candlelight and splendor. Hidden in the wardrobe is SIR RICHARD B., a promising writer and expert voyeur. He recorded the following events.

KING HENRY
Thank you for meeting me here, me lady.

ANNE BOLEYN
It is an honor and a privilege to be in the presence of your Grace. I feel a gratitude deep in my veins.

KING HENRY
Well, I hope that I can transform that gratitude into desire.

ANNE BOLEYN (BLUSHING)
My lord, there is a yearning for you that pumps through my blood from my heart to my fingers to my toes to my . . .

KING HENRY
To your what?

ANNE BOLEYN
To my, my . . .

KING HENRY
Say it!

ANNE BOLEYN
My virginal lady button.
Anne Boleyn starts to fake-cry from embarrassment.

ANNE BOLEYN (CONT'D)
I can't believe I said that! I'm a monster!
King Henry leans forward and lays a bejeweled hand on her fragile shoulder.

KING HENRY
My lady, it is that very button that I intend to push, and push, and push . . .
And with that he plants a long kiss on Anne's open wet mouth. Both pull back and gasp for air.

KING HENRY (CONT'D)
Did I bite your tongue?

ANNE BOLEYN
No, your Grace.

KING HENRY
I tasted blood.

ANNE BOLEYN
I did just eat a freshly killed calf.
Anne pulls out a piece of bloody beef from her cheek.

ANNE BOLEYN (CONT'D)
I believe this belongs to you.
King Henry takes it.

KING HENRY
Thank you.
King Henry chews it slowly as Anne watches. A long GROWL escapes Sir Richard's stomach.

ANNE BOLEYN
What was that?

SIR RICHARD (WHISPERING)
Oh Holy Ghost!

KING HENRY
Could be an owl getting drunk in the moonlight, maybe an angel defecating on a cloud, or perhaps my lust for you becoming audible.

ANNE BOLEYN
Well, if it is the third, then it is the noise that I have been waiting to hear since I pushed through my mother's thighs.

KING HENRY
Then come be serenaded by your destiny. Rawwwer!
Anne giggles with delight and falls into King Henry's open arms. Sir Richard is dripping with sweat but can still shakily write this. King Henry proceeds to rip Anne's clothes to shreds growling like an animal while she screeches like a banshee who loves animals.

KING HENRY
Now show me that BUTTON!

Anne takes her cue and removes her corset. She is standing completely in the nude. Her tits are pointed like witches' hats in the damp chill of the chamber. She has a soft plump tummy like creamy vanilla pudding, and below that, betwixt her full thighs is a dense forest of hair. It is tangled in parts, and hangs to mid-thigh, gorgeous and glistening.

KING HENRY (CONT'D)

Oh sweet heaven!

King Henry runs to Anne and pushes his face into her thatch of pubic hair. He immediately reels back.

KING HENRY (CONT'D)

Oh God!

ANNE BOLEYN

What is it, my King?

KING HENRY

I'm not sure. I went to taste the honeys of your sweet nest, but was overcome by the sulfurlike smell of Satan! I'm afraid! Perhaps Satan is in the room with us, chaperoning this sinful tryst!

ANNE BOLEYN

I'm afraid too! Let me smell it.

Anne bends down and takes in her scent.

ANNE BOLEYN (CONT'D)

I don't smell anything unusual, that is just me. Here, let me help you get closer to my button.

Anne pulls back handfuls of hair. As she does a fly or two escapes from the knots. Soon she is revealing a sweet pink button covered in a layer of protective dirt and oil.

KING HENRY (HOLDING HIS NOSE)

It's beautiful.

ANNE BOLEYN

It is my gift to you, my lord. Just don't tell anyone we did it before we were married.

KING HENRY

It will not be recorded.

Sir Richard silently snickers from the wardrobe while enduring a swelling in his lap from the sight of Anne's pink button. It is quite beautiful, unlike the buttons that Sir Richard has experienced in his past, which all seemed to be inflamed and dripping down like a turkey gobble.

ANNE BOLEYN

Then come have the feast that is my body!

King Henry takes a deep breath and goes in for a taste of the button.

KING HENRY

It is tangy! But I am going to make myself love it!

Anne moans with pleasure as she falls back onto the bed. King Henry sucks until he can no longer breathe and comes up for hungry gulps of fresh air. Anne writhes a bit and then grabs his codpiece and pulls it to her mouth.

ANNE BOLEYN

Now I'm hungry for you.

KING HENRY

Well, you shall have what you crave.

He carefully pulls on the codpiece but is unable to remove it. In a moment of panic and frustration he calls out to his servants.

KING HENRY (CONT'D)

Servants! Remove garments for copulation and sleeping!

From the shadows THREE SERVANTS emerge and quickly remove all of King Henry's garments. Anne modestly throws a bearskin over her flesh and waits patiently.

KING HENRY (CONT'D)

Enough! You can leave. Wait. Anne, do you want anything?

ANNE BOLEYN

I'd love a calf burger.

KING HENRY

Get that for her! But most important, leave now!

The servants leave and King Henry lies down next to Anne, as naked as she. His body is large, circular on top with two tiny legs sticking out like a caramel apple. He is shiny like one as well. He pulls on his sausage manhood.

KING HENRY (CONT'D)

Care for a taste?

ANNE BOLEYN

Would I ever! I'm starving!

Anne eagerly crawls on all fours down to the crown jewels. She carefully lowers her head and her tongue to the prize. Her head snaps up.

ANNE BOLEYN (CONT'D)
Oh!

KING HENRY
What is it?

ANNE BOLEYN
I smell it too! The sulfurlike smell of Satan that was with us before. Only this time he must have brought his dinner with him. A rotting sauerkraut dinner, one that has been soaking in the feces- and corpse-riddled moat. I've never inhaled anything like it. One deep breath and I think I am in Hell's pantry.

KING HENRY (CALLING OUT TO THE ROOM)
Damn you, Satan! How dare you come here chomping on your foul dinner, ruining our union! We are meant to be together, by God! We will fornicate in your face, Satan! IN YOUR EVIL FACE!

ANNE BOLEYN
That's right, Satan! Chew with your mouth closed!

KING HENRY
Come here, Anne!
Anne crawls up to King Henry and lowers herself onto his noble shaft.

KING HENRY (CONT'D)
Stop! Stop! What are you doing?

ANNE BOLEYN
I'm becoming one with you, my lord.

KING HENRY
Not like that! No one mounts the King! I'm on top, always!

ANNE BOLEYN
My apologies, your Grace. It is I who should be rode.

KING HENRY
That's the spirit, you gorgeous mare!
King Henry flips Anne onto her back and jabs her middle area with his fleshy sword.

KING HENRY (CONT'D)

I can't find the special hole! Servants!

The servants rush back into the room. Two of them pull back Anne's thick pelvic hair while the other knowingly guides the King's sword into its sacred sheath.

KING HENRY (CONT'D)

There we go.

As they exit one of the servants carefully places a calf burger near Anne's mouth. The King, now in place, lowers his body onto Anne's to commence his thrusting.

ANNE BOLEYN (GASPING AND CHEWING CALF BURGER)

Oh, my lord!

KING HENRY

I know. It is everything that I had thought it would be as well (grunt). All those secret smiles (grunt), all the casual fondling (grunt), the time I had to talk to the pope with an erection because I was thinking of you (grunt, grunt).

ANNE BOLEYN

My lord, I'm afraid you are crushing my lungs with your divine grace!

KING HENRY

No worries, I am done. My seed has been spilt inside you. Something about the pope's face made my seed spill.

King Henry climbs off Anne as she takes her first breath of air since the fornication.

KING HENRY (CONT'D)

Servants! Fetch my lover an outfit from my soon-to-be ex-wife's wardrobe!

Servants' footsteps are heard coming toward the wardrobe that Sir Richard now realizes is the Queen's. His erection retracts inside him like a turtle as he realizes that he will soon be drawn and quartered. In a last-ditch effort to save himself he hides his manuscript inside the pocket of a cloak and pretends to sleep . . .

CHAPTER 3

Cupid's Toolbox

Tools of the Trade When Trading Bodily Fluids

The talent that makes humans better at carpentry than the rest of the animal kingdom is also what makes us better lovers: our ability to use **tools**. Without them, man is helpless, armed only with his fingernails and his wits. But with them, he can perform all manner of orgasmic wonders, from scratching a nagging sexual itch just out of reach to building an entire city of love shacks.

If you learn one thing from this chapter, it should be that there's *no shame* in using **marital aids**.* Latex vaginas, butt plugs, penis pumps, and coconut-flavored lubes that get warm and tingly when you blow on them are the bedside friends that let humans live up to their full sexual potential. In fact, when it comes to sex toys, the only shame is *not* using them. Because when you say no to pocket rockets, blow-up dolls, chinstrap dildos, and custom-made Swedish sex furniture, not only are you missing out on a good time, you're ignoring three thousand years of erotic trial and error, carried out by brave men and women who put their genitals on the line so *you* could have more fun in the sack. A lot of hard work went into sex toys, so don't turn your back on them. Or better yet . . . *do*.

The **sextant**, *an early sex toy that allowed sailors to calibrate both the angle of the dangle (°D) and the motion of the ocean (M)*

Perhaps the greatest sex toy of all is Knowledge, the sex toy of the mind. For that reason, this chapter also includes proven pickup lines, sexy mood setters, and personal grooming tips GUARANTEED to get you into a situation where sex could conceivably happen. To put it bluntly (the preferred method when it comes to sex toys), this chapter has everything you need to turn you into a boner-fide SEX MACHINE.

(Except batteries.)

---

* The preferred term among people who are too shy to say "sex toys," but who don't mind saying "aids" in a sexual context.

APHRODISIACS
Scale of Effectiveness

BO-OI-OI-OI-ING!

Five years of nothing but prison slop

Ground unicorn horn
(absorbed rectally)

Wife Lover's Pizza

Anything sold next to a cash register

Spanish fly

Chocolate-covered oysters

Oysters

Chocolate

British fly

LESS EFFECTIVE

Augmentooming
(Augmentation and Grooming)

If you want to have sex, you're going to have to put your best foot forward. And if that foot happens to be a freshly shorn scrotum or luscious triple-D boob, that will only help your chances. Fortunately, advances in medical science and the hygienic arts can make you not just doable, but *must-doable*.

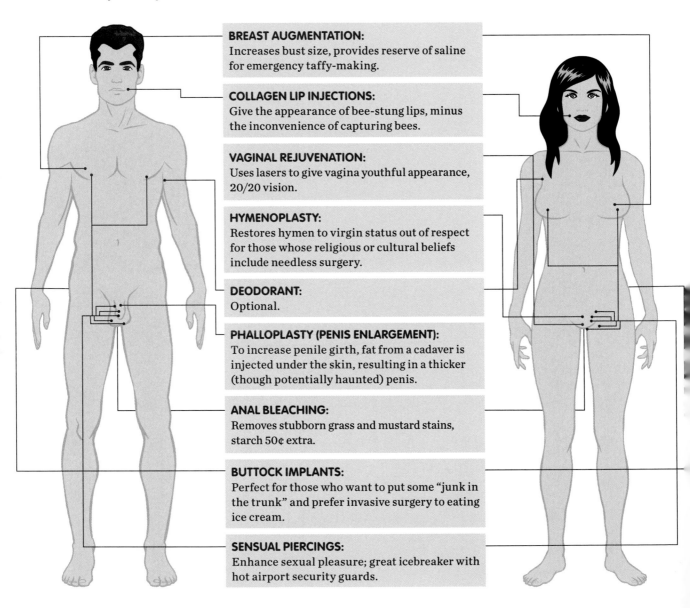

BREAST AUGMENTATION:
Increases bust size, provides reserve of saline for emergency taffy-making.

COLLAGEN LIP INJECTIONS:
Give the appearance of bee-stung lips, minus the inconvenience of capturing bees.

VAGINAL REJUVENATION:
Uses lasers to give vagina youthful appearance, 20/20 vision.

HYMENOPLASTY:
Restores hymen to virgin status out of respect for those whose religious or cultural beliefs include needless surgery.

DEODORANT:
Optional.

PHALLOPLASTY (PENIS ENLARGEMENT):
To increase penile girth, fat from a cadaver is injected under the skin, resulting in a thicker (though potentially haunted) penis.

ANAL BLEACHING:
Removes stubborn grass and mustard stains, starch 50¢ extra.

BUTTOCK IMPLANTS:
Perfect for those who want to put some "junk in the trunk" and prefer invasive surgery to eating ice cream.

SENSUAL PIERCINGS:
Enhance sexual pleasure; great icebreaker with hot airport security guards.

Pubescaping

Letting your short and curlies grow wild may have been acceptable back in the sixties, when you needed a place to hide your weed and communist propaganda. But the modern lover is expected to trim his or her bush like the eightcenth green at St. Andrews. Typically, men shave their pubic hair to make their penises look BIGGER, while women style their muffs to make their vaginas appear _{smaller.}

The Titanic

Giant redwood

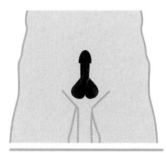

A smaller penis

Snowflake

An ant

Lithium atom

> **FUCKTOID**
> According to legend, Dutch settlers bought Fire Island from the Indians for a **handful of anal beads.**

PICKUP LINES
for Every Conceivable Situation

IF YOU JUST PERFORMED THE HEIMLICH MANEUVER ON SOMEONE

If I were that chicken bone, I wouldn't have wanted to come out, either.

BIRTHDAY PARTY

Are you a birthday candle? Because I'd like to blow you until I get my wish.

MAGIC SHOW, OR IN A PARK WHERE MAGICIANS SOMETIMES PERFORM

Are you a magician? Because I think you might make my penis disappear into your vagina/anus!

CONSTRUCTION SITE

Are you the building inspector? Because I'd like you to assess the durability of my erection.

IF YOU JUST DELIVERED A BABY IN THE BACKSEAT OF A CAB

Say you'll get dinner with me or I'll put it back.

IF YOU JUST PERFORMED CPR ON SOMEONE

I just saved your life. Will you save me a dance?

GROCERY STORE, BAKED GOODS AISLE

Can I squeeze your buns? Because I'd like to determine whether or not I want to put my meat inside them.

IN LINE AT THE DMV

I think my heart has Stockholm syndrome because you captured it and it doesn't want to come home.

INTEROFFICE ROMANCE, CHANCE MEETING IN STATIONERY CLOSET

Are you a pink eraser? Because I'd like to make a mistake and rub you all over.

AT A DIFFERENT MAGIC SHOW

Are you related to Criss Angel? Because you look like an Angel.

INTEROFFICE ROMANCE, PRINTING HOUSE

Are you a typesetter? Because I'd like to examine your colon before your next period.

IF YOU'RE PRINCE WILLIAM

I'm Prince William.

ALL OTHER SITUATIONS

You better call 911 because my fantasy just mugged my wildest dreams. Also, I'm staring at a suspicious love package left by a sex terrorist!

Various Methods of Contraception, Demonstrated on a Banana

CONDOMS

Place the condom at the top of the banana. Pinch the reservoir tip between your thumb and index finger, and use your free hand to roll the condom over the banana. Quickly, now! That banana is getting softer by the second.

THE PILL

Consult with your doctor to find the birth control pill that's right for your banana. Then, diligently give the banana a pill every day around the same time. Some of the pills are placebos, but you should still mash them into your banana just so you stay in the routine.

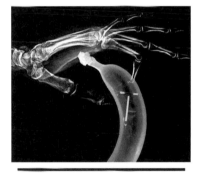

CONTRACEPTIVE SPONGE

Combining barrier and spermicidal methods of contraception, this form of birth control can even be used to clean up the mess afterwards.

INTRAUTERINE METHODS (IUDS)

Lasting anywhere from five to twelve years, this T-shaped baby-stopper must be inserted into your banana by a licensed fruit doctor.

SURGICAL STERILIZATION

Eliminates the need for birth control, but after it's done, who honestly wants that banana?

WITHDRAWAL METHOD

The oldest and least reliable form of birth control, "pulling out" requires removing your banana at the last possible moment.

ABSTINENCE

The most surefire way of not having a baby is never unpeeling your banana, no matter how much you want to.

ANAL SEX

Not the most enjoyable method for getting your banana, but better than no banana at all.

The **BEST $ELLING SEX TOYS** of all Time

HORNY HORNY HIPPOS

Spank your lever as fast as you can . . . you'll be surprised how many balls you can fit in your mouth!

Rubik's PUBES

This puzzling pile of pubes is a cock-teaser as well as a brainteaser.

Sleazy Bake OVEN

Makes erotic cakes so hot, you won't believe they were cooked with a lightbulb.

Cabbage Snatch Kids

Popular and often in short supply, these collectible cuties can get even the most finicky fornicators eating their vegetables.

Gay-Doh

It's here, it's queer . . . get used to picking it out of your shag carpet.

Teddy FUXPIN

A VHS slot on Teddy's back lets this animatronic accessory lip-sync to the satisfied groans of your favorite porno.

Can't make it to the dildo store?

Some household objects can double as sex objects. But be careful!

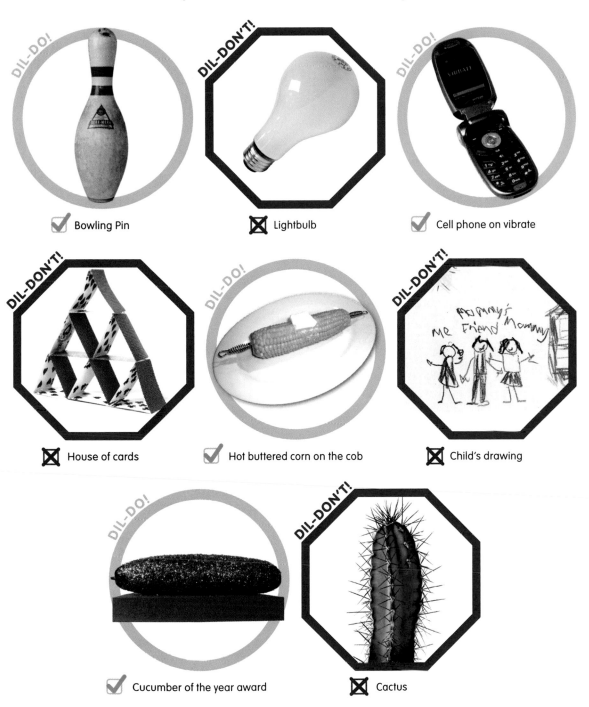

DIL-DO! ☑ Bowling Pin

DIL-DON'T! ☒ Lightbulb

DIL-DO! ☑ Cell phone on vibrate

DIL-DON'T! ☒ House of cards

DIL-DO! ☑ Hot buttered corn on the cob

DIL-DON'T! ☒ Child's drawing

DIL-DO! ☑ Cucumber of the year award

DIL-DON'T! ☒ Cactus

The Sexiest Song Ever Written

Whether bringing a date back to your apartment or simply to the backseat of your car, the right music can turn awkward silence into a lip-and-tongue symphony. For this reason, seduction experts have spent countless hours trying to compile the ultimate make-out mix. This is a complete waste of time.

The truth is you need only one song for seduction. Written in 1974, "Gimme All Your ████" was banned after its first broadcast resulted in thousands of embarrassing, involuntary orgasms and three forklift crashes. This is the first time it has been reproduced, with the sexiest notes and lyrics redacted for safety.

Gimme All Your ████

A Note from the Authors

When we agreed to write this book, we had only one condition—we wouldn't discuss any specifics of our own sex lives. This is for three reasons:

First, we don't know you.

Second, we have parents who happen to be alive *and* literate. So just the fact that we're writing a sex book is enough to make Christmas awkward.

Third and most important, we have the best sex of anybody in the world. If the government learns of our superhuman lovemaking abilities, they will most certainly bring us in for testing. And we only want to use our sensual powers for good.

Nonetheless, we had a personal anecdote that fit so perfectly with the theme of this chapter that we decided to lift our veil of modesty, if only for a few pages. So unless you happen to be our parents, please enjoy this peek into an actual event that happened to us last summer. And if the government does harness the energy from our lovemaking to power a death ray, well, we hope it was worth it.

The Cock Ring of Quetzalcoatl

We were nine days deep into an archaeological dig where we were working as professional bone-dusters. As each precious fossil rose up from the earth's tomb it had to be rubbed down impeccably from top to bottom. No one was better at doing this than us.

In Mexico City a secret chamber had been discovered under the ancient Templo Mayor. The purpose of the room, located in the southeast corner of the temple, was a mystery. Among piles of human bones were two partially intact skeletons frozen in the missionary position. It was these skeletons that we were cleaning. Each bone of the eternally horny pair had to be wiped down. It was intricate work, and by the end of the day our aching bodies were willing to trade places with them if it meant we could get a margarita.

Just as Kristen was about to clock out Rich pulled her aside.

"I found something." Rich had a mischievous twinkle in his eye, and Kristen looked down to see him holding what appeared to be an ancient cock ring. "I found it under the two skeletons. It must have fallen off the male when his erection finally gave way to black putrefaction."

Kristen, who has a weakness for antique cock rings, glanced at the other archaeologists in the tomb. "Well, we can't legally remove it from the site."

"No, we can't. But we can work overtime tonight."

And with that we waited for the last archaeologist to leave, telling each departing colleague we were going to bone-dust for another hour or two and then we'd join everyone for tequila shots at Pato Afortunado. Soon we were the only two on the site.

We'd made intimate love in public before, but never in front of skeletons. We were ready to give those empty eye sockets a show their brainless skulls would never forget nor remember. Kissing and sucking ensued in superb and perfect ways, and before long we were ready for the big event. Kristen held up the Aztec cock ring. "It's beautiful."

The piece was made out of smooth marble and featured a meticulous carving of an Aztec couple using the cock ring. Rich pursed his full, pouty lips and blew a stubborn cobweb from the artifact. "It looks like there's a message written in Nahuatl. Let me get my translation book."

Kristen held Rich in place. "Are you kidding? I'm ready for you now." With that, the cock ring's six hundred years of dusty celibacy came to an end as we screwed it onto Rich's well-endowed and classically beautiful member. Rich's unit was a perfect match for Kristen's timelessly rugged passion trap, and turning her around, he found himself caught in it yet again.

We began to make love, but somehow things felt different. It was still the same incredible journey of exploring layer upon layer of seemingly unattainable ecstasy that we usually have, but this time the earth moved literally instead of just figuratively. We looked down and saw the ground vibrating as the evening light transformed into a sharp orange glow. Our ears were overcome with a loud moan that seemed to come from the belly of the earth.

"What's happening?" Kristen tried to scream over it.

"I don't know, but every time I pump you things change even more!" Rich hollered back.

It was true: as we boned, the scenery continued to change. The chamber became new again, the bones picked themselves up and grew muscles, skin, and hair, and instantly they were walking around as actual living beings. In a flash, the skeletons we had been dusting morphed into two beautiful Aztec adults in the middle of making love. They instantly realized their cock ring was gone, and that we had it. They began screaming at us in Nahuatl, but their yells were swallowed by a wall of dust as the chamber disintegrated, taking the angry Aztecs with it. We suddenly found ourselves in the middle of an untamed jungle, silent except for the the chirps of critters and the rhythmic clicks of the cock ring.

"Rich! Stop making love for just one second."

"One second is too long."

"I agree . . . half a second." Rich reluctantly paused and Kristen turned around. "I think we've gone back in time!"

This was tremendous, especially for two professional archaeologists. We had spent years picking through the remains of lost eras, imagining what they looked like alive, pressing their dirt to our faces to catch any lasting scent, and now we were smelling and seeing it all brand-new. But at the same time, we were very horny.

"Is it because we fucked through the sound barrier and ultimately the time barrier?"

"I've fucked you harder. This cock ring must have powers. See if you can read the inscription."

Kristen bent down to the read the cock ring, her gorgeous ass creating a heart silhouette in the prehistoric moonlight.

"It says, 'Those who don the ring of the Quetzalco-mmmmmmmm mmmmmm——'" Kristen's mouth slid over Rich's engorged shaft out of habit.

At that moment, a group of brutish, hairy cavemen emerged from the jungle. They instantly spotted us and readied their spears, confusing our hairless white bodies for the aliens who were always trying to get them to build pyramids in their honor. Rich frantically tugged at the cock ring, but it was held firmly in place by his thick man-flesh. "We've got to get this thing off of me!"

"Hold on, let me finish reading the inscription." Kristen fixed her gaze on the ancient symbols and concentrated on using her mouth for translating instead of pleasure. "'Those who don the ring of Quetzalcoatl shall go back to the beginning. The only way to return to the present is through the power of an orgasmmmmmmmmmmmmmm——'"

The temptation of Rich's rigid cock once again proved too much for Kristen, but they got the idea. "Okay, babe, looks like we're going to have to keep doing what we do best to get home." Rich hoisted Kristen onto on his aching rod, and not a moment too soon. One of the undoubtedly turned-on cavemen had hurled a spear at them, but when the humping resumed the spear froze in the air, then returned to the hand that threw it, like a caveman movie playing in reverse. With a squeeze of Kristen's ample breast the Neanderthals turned into furry babies, then disappeared completely.

We were safe but no closer to getting back home. Kristen locked her feet around Rich's legs and rocked his cock as hard as she could——so hard she reached an orgasm that made her shriek like a wild animal. Unfortunately, Rich wasn't the only one who heard it. From the tops of the trees a *Tyrannosaurus rex* lifted its head and zeroed in on its prey. "Oh my God! Rich, you have to cum!"

Rich desperately wanted to, if only to release the growing pressure from his imprisoned schlong. But it wasn't happening. The dinosaur ripped through tree trunks with its massive jaw and made its way toward us. Rich flipped Kristen over and pounded her with all his might. Upside down, Kristen could see the remains of a pterodactyl still stuck in the monster's giant teeth. Being so close to death plus Rich's panicked thrusting caused her to explode a second time. But Rich remained rock-hard and orgasm-free.

"This cock ring is too good!" Rich yelled, half pleased and half doomed. Just as we were about to go spelunking in the carnivore's horrific mouth cave the earth vibrated again, and when the dust cleared we were on the side of a red-hot volcano.

"I guess we went back even further." Rich pinned Kristen to the side of the volcano and continued to give it to her from behind. Kristen felt the heat emanating from the molten rock and realized it couldn't match the friction inside her. "Ahhh, man, Rich, this volcano is going to erupt any minute, and so am I!"

Rich's cock had never felt so good. The tightness of the ring and the sheer adrenaline of the situation were bringing him to the edge of ecstasy. But the ring's powers refused to let him get off easy.

Kristen, however, was a different story. Rich heard her scream and saw the lava pour from the crater at the same time. At first he wasn't sure if it was a scream of terror, but when he felt her love canal ripple and tighten around him, he knew it was all because of him.

"Baby, I'm going for three, are you getting any closer? Because we are about to melt like Velveeta!" Rich laid Kristen down and rode all the way back in time, to the very beginning. We felt the hot earth cool under us and break apart, until we were fucking on a lonely asteroid like an X-rated version of *The Little Prince*. The red sky became a black wash, the sound of our slapping genitals echoing in the abyss of the newly formed universe. Soon, the universe itself was smaller than Rich's bulging hard-on.

Our bodies grew numb with each breath. We knew it was just a matter of time before we became victims of erotic space asphyxiation. Luckily, Kristen remembered a trick. She took one of Rich's ice-cold nipples into her teeth and bit down on it, hard. The shocking sensation was exactly what Rich needed to cum. As Kristen felt his cock swell her nerves gave into ecstasy yet again, but this time on an even greater scale. The combination of her quivering and the warm blood trickling down his chest caused every cell in Rich's body to explode in jubilation. It was the most overwhelming orgasm of our lives.

At the same time, the sole pinpoint of light that was our infant universe exploded in every direction, millions of pieces scattering across the gaping void. In nanoseconds, the glowing shards coagulated into stars and planets. Before we realized what was happening, we found ourselves back on Earth, clinging to each other in the musty tomb. A single space icicle clung to Rich's still-hard nipple.

The magical cock ring fell to the floor with a clang and rolled back to its rightful skeleton owners. Kristen was speechless from her quadruple orgasm that had spanned billions of years. Rich had only one thing to say: "Now that was a big bang."

Dedicated to Dr. Joycelyn Elders
"The Galileo of Masturbation"

CHAPTER 4

Masturbation:

The Auto-Erotic Fixation

Masturbation:
The Auto-Erotic Fixation

A sign of a great species is being able to meet a basic need by just being yourself. Turtles carry shelter on their backs. Silkworms make their own scarves. And humans, in yet another display of our evolutionary brilliance, can fulfill the greatest need of all: fending off the hornies. We do it by **wanking off**.

The hardest part of Anne Geddes' job is getting the babies to stop masturbating.

Though masturbating is often vilified as "dirty" or "sinful" or "something you shouldn't do at a fancy restaurant," it is actually one of the greatest gifts we can give ourselves. It is exercise, yet it feels good. You get to use your imagination, but you don't have to buy any expensive construction paper or finger paints. And best of all, any guilt you have afterward can be wiped away with more masturbating. Both "whittling the whalebone" and "polishing the pearl" are so ingrained in our DNA that infants have been known to handle their business long before it's open for business. And as the old saying goes, "If babies do it, it can't be bad." But there was a time when people didn't masturbate. Not surprisingly, it was in biblical times.

After the embarrassing sexual fiasco that was Adam and Eve, God issued an emergency recall of all humans. He shortened our arms so that our longest finger could barely reach our belly buttons, enough for lint management but nothing more. Making our arms any longer would only spell TROUBLE in giant capital letters of wasted semen.

Surprisingly, not jerking off made people even bigger jerk-offs. God was about to erase our species altogether and just start from scratch when he saw Noah, still in bed at 1 p.m. Not only was he five hundred years old, his arms had been stretched out to the unthinkable length of below the waist in a tug-o'-war accident. Yet despite this deformity, Noah was more relaxed and easy to deal with than most humans (though he did go through a lot of hand lotion). Right there on the spot, God decided to start over with Noah as his new prototype.

For a guy who supposedly cared about animals, Noah loved choking his chicken.

God commanded Noah to build an ark in preparation for a great flood that would rid the world of non-wankers once and for all. After only a hundred years of hard labor (and equally hard masturbating), Noah completed his task. The waters came, and so did Noah. And when the waters receded, Noah was a ready to replace it with a veritable deluge of ready-made, long-armed-person sperm. And it was **Good**.

Masturfiction:
Five Myths about Masturbation

The number of misconceptions about masturbating is almost equal to the number of people doing it at this very moment (which is a lot). But before you begin exploring your uncharted territories, it's important to separate fact from friction:

MYTH
Masturbating gives you acne.

FACT
Masturbating does *not* give you acne. It only appears that way, since people with acne typically can't get a date and have to masturbate all the time.

MYTH
If you masturbate too much, you will use up all your semen.

FACT
Semen is a renewable resource. But you should be saving it anyway. We recommend Tupperware and an industrial freezer. Don't forget to label!

MYTH
Masturbating will stunt your growth.

FACT
Actually, it increases growth. The same chemicals that make your penis or clitoris grow during masturbation naturally spill into other parts of your body, making them bigger too. Anytime you see a tall person, you can be sure they jerk off all the time.

MYTH
Masturbating can make you go blind.

FACT
While this is usually dismissed as an old wives' tale, studies suggest masturbation-induced blindness is indeed possible. If you have recently masturbated and notice a sudden decrease in vision, it is imperative that you immediately rinse your eyes with a mixture of water, hydrogen

MYTH
Masturbating gives you hairy palms.

FACT
This one is true. Growing hair is the body's natural defense against hand chafing. Fortunately, there are plenty of options for the fuzzy-fingered. (SEE "Things You Can Do With Hairy Palms," page 69.)

Things You Shouldn't Think About While Masturbating

One of the best things about masturbating is that you can let your imagination roam as freely as your hands. But when directing your own mental porno, some scenes are best left on the cutting room floor. Try not to think about:

- Your grandmother
- Your grandmother masturbating
- The millions of germs on your hand
- Genocide
- How easy it would be for someone to secretly install a Web cam in your bedroom
- How the water you're wasting could supply a village in Africa (in shower only)
- How they'd find you if you died right now
- Yams
- Frankenstein naked
- How they took *The Tonight Show* away from Conan
- How you are just an insignificant speck in the universe
- A word that rhymes with "orange"
- Cancer
- *"Ziggy"*

- How much cash you just blew on that terrible blind date
- The death of your first pet
- Where homeless people masturbate
- The Trail of Tears
- The ceiling
- How you never followed your dreams

Depending how you look at it, this image is either primo wank material or a total boner killer.

DO WOMEN MASTURBATE?

One of the biggest myths about masturbation is that women just aren't that into it. This simply isn't true. Behind every strong masturbator, there's an even stronger missturbator. Women just happen to go about it differently.

	MEN	WOMEN
IDEAL SETTING	Anywhere	On silk sheets covered with rose petals, surrounded by scented candles, with smooth jazz playing
DURATION	As quickly as possible	Three minutes to however long it takes to realize you're dying of dehydration
FREQUENCY	As often as possible	Precisely 330.47 Hz (also known as the HIGH setting)
ORGASM COMPARABLE TO	A satisfying bowel movement out of your penis	That shiver you feel before you sneeze, only the shiver is pure ecstasy and the sneeze is touching the face of God
CLEANUP	YES	Just the rose petals

Things You Can Do with Hairy Palms

Wash your car

Put on puppet shows

Hand-model for niche products

THE LEGEND OF
PAGE 69

Whether you read classic literature or coloring books, you can always count on one page to be sexier than the rest: page 69. Don't believe it? Look for yourself. In the Holy Bible, page 69 just happens to be where Moses and the Pharaoh compare rods. In *Moby-Dick*, it's where Mrs. Hussey offers both Ishmael and Queequeg a taste of her succulent clam chowder. And in *The Essential Calvin and Hobbes* . . . well, let's just say it inspired a lot of bumper stickers. Time and again, page 69 is practically begging to wind up stuck to page 68. Why is this?

Some say that authors see the little "6" going down on that little "9" in the corner of the page and it subconsciously inspires them. Others claim that publishers got wind of the "always sex on page 69" legend and started pimping out the pre-70 mark, just to avoid disappointing prospective book buyers. Whatever the reason, you're probably wondering why this page 69 doesn't seem all that sexy. That's because our "6" and "9" have fucked right off the page. Watch out for the wet spot.

Masturpiece Theatre:
Role-Playing for One

THE TICKING TIME BOMB

What you'll need:

- A chair
- Some rope
- A digital clock
- Some paper towel rolls painted red (save the paper towels for cleanup!)

The scene:

A madman has taken you hostage and tied you to a chair. To make matters worse, he's rigged a bomb that will detonate unless you give yourself an orgasm before the timer reaches zero. Which will come first: the little death or the big one?

ALIEN ZOO

What you'll need:

- A jail cell
- A Dixie cup wrapped in tinfoil
- Some space hay

The scene:

Earth has been destroyed and you are the sole survivor. It's up to you to produce viable semen for alien scientists so they can reconstitute the human race. Also, alien zoo attendance is way down and a masturbating earthling exhibit would probably sell some tickets.

STATE OF YOUR UNION

What you'll need:

- A podium
- A message
- Some people who look like Congress members

The scene:

You have won the presidency, but it was a tough race and you need to let off some steam. With your crotch hidden behind the podium it may be the only time the Secret Service agents don't have their eyes on it. Can you deliver the State of the Union address and discreetly pleasure yourself at the same time?

THAR'S GOLD IN THEM THAR GENITALS!

What you'll need:

- Prospector hat
- A pie plate with a hole in the bottom
- Some elbow grease

The scene:

Word has spread about a mighty big lode . . . in your pants! You've got to grab the main vein before any claim jumpers steal your precious nuggets. Start shaking that pan and go for the gold!

FUCKTOID

One of most fervent opponents of masturbation was **John Harvey Kellogg**, doctor and co-inventor of corn flakes cereal. Kellogg advocated using bandages, acid, shock therapy, and even genital cages to prevent adolescents from pleasuring themselves, which makes it all the more surprising that his cereal featured a giant cock on the box.

*John Harvey Kellogg thought life should be as **bland and joyless** as his cereal.*

'Bating Blunders

Walking in on someone in the act of self-appreciation can be mortifying for all parties involved—so much so that Frances Calhoun made a living writing a syndicated advice column based solely on masturbation etiquette. "Whoopsie Daisy!" ran for decades, and at the height of its popularity was translated into forty-three different languages. Ms. Calhoun graciously lent us some of her favorite questions and responses.

B8 | THE SEXY SEX DAILY CHRONICLE ☆☆☆☆☆

Whoopsie Daisy!

by Frances Calhoun

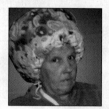

Dear Frances,
As a strong, single mother of a fifteen-year-old boy I thought I was able to handle anything. Until now! I walked in on my son, Reginald D. Gatherer, rubbing his penis wildly while tonguing a glossy poster of Alyssa Milano. I didn't know what to do, so I screamed, and then he screamed, and then I told him that I made his favorite lasagna, and he said he'd be out in a minute, and I said it's getting cold, and he said he'd be right out, and the whole time I didn't know where to look, so I just stared into those beady Alyssa Milano eyes, and they were staring right back at me, and it was like I could read her mind, and it said: I f**ked your son! What do I do?

Scared,

Lacey Gatherer

Dear Lacey,
Gracious, that sounds dreadful! I certainly hope your lasagna wasn't spoiled. Those Italian casseroles can turn into a soggy mess. Still, the whole situation could have been avoided. Here are some basic guidelines to ensure the only noodle you see is on your dinner fork.

Rule number one: always knock. That is the Frances Calhoun golden rule! When the Lord takes me to heaven I will write that on my gravestone. Here Lies Frances Calhoun, Please Knock!

> **"... I didn't know what to do, so I screamed, and then he screamed, and then I told him that I made his favorite lasagna..."**

Because I will be up in heaven "strumming my harp," if you know what I mean. But I digress, I'm not dead and neither is your son! (Which is surprising. Most teenagers would be suicidal if their mother walked in on them, then wrote a letter about it using their full name to a very popular column. My second piece of advice is to put a lock on your aspirin bottle!)

But most important: get rid of Alyssa Milano. There's nothing wrong with Reginald pulling the ripcord of his pleasure parachute now and again. But Alyssa Milano is dangerous. My bridge partner Dotty heard she has a tail! A tail!!! It's so crazy it has to be true! "Who's the Boss?" you ask? My guess is Old Scratch himself!

Dear Frances,

I have been a flight attendant since the days when you could light up and bring a gallon of gasoline into the cabin, no questions asked! We were just having fun. And I do miss those times, but they are over and now it's time to be scared. Which is why I was so frightened when I went to the cockpit to see if the captain wanted a cup of coffee only to find him with one hand on the airplane's yoke and the other hand on his! All I could do was pretend that it wasn't happening. Should I have said something? We had a perfect landing.

Flying high,

Cheryl

Dear Cheryl,
My goodness! What an exciting life you steward-esses have. Whooshing through the clouds all day long like angels. And I can just imagine your pilot gazing down at this beautiful earth, so close to the sky he can touch God, oh but not quite! But he can certainly come close by touching himself. Boy, I'd buff my button too. I can certainly sympathize with your preoccupied pilot. Especially since you didn't follow my number-one rule: always knock! The door's not going to complain!

Poetry Corner

And now for the Whoopsie Daisy Frances Calhoun Poetry Corner! Please enjoy this week's poems.

The Man Who Masturbated Too Much
There once was a man who choked his chicken

The one between his legs

It came back to life and he choked it again

For days and days and days

The people in town didn't hear from him

They chalked it up to malaise

Until that fateful evening

He walked out in the street in a daze

He held up the chicken he was beating

It turned out it was his dick.

The Woman Who Wanked Wred
There once was a lady who polished her pearl

She did so since she was a little girl

She rubbed it for years to make it shinier

Her skin growing pale and her muscles tinier

Years went by and she went into seclusion

Suitors were turned away in confusion

This precious pearl must be an illusion

Finally she announced the jewel was on sale

And everyone gasped at the big unveil

The pearl was her clit, but rubbed raw
   like a ruby

"World Masturbation Day"

Janie sipped her martini and tried to look comfortable being alone at the bar. She laid out the paper in front of her and stared at the headline.

"WORLD MASTURBATION DAY A DAY AWAY"

It was all anyone was talking about. Could it top last year? All the wars ended, at least for a day. Janie scanned the bar. She was alone with the bartender and Wolf Blitzer chatting incessantly on the tube.

> *"What you're watching now is a clip from Sudan. As you can see, the rebel soldiers have put down their guns and picked up their dongs. World Masturbation Day is already under way on that side of the world. It's a beautiful thing—the only day the world can breathe easy, and heavy."*

A chubby man sat down next to Janie. She quickly buried herself in the paper to avoid conversation.

> The government still has no answer for the sudden vibrator crisis. Manufacturers have completely sold out, and it looks like some women may be without them for World Masturbation Day.

Janie patted the vibrator in her purse. Last year was the first time she masturbated. She always felt too reserved to touch herself, but when the whole world came out to do it she gave in to peer pressure. It was so wonderful she couldn't wait to do it again this year. She gulped the last of her martini.

The fat man took his cue. "Buy you another?"

She glanced at his face. He had a double chin, tiny eyes, and a thin greasy hairline. Wolf filled the awkward silence with another update.

"The President is banking on the release of the recession, follow-ing the release of six billion orgasms."

"Another martini?"

Janie shook her head. "No thanks, it's late." She started to fold her paper.

"Am I too ugly?" His forwardness startled her.

"No, I didn't even notice, I—oh shit!" She dropped her purse, spilling its contents on the cement floor. Janie was mortified as the vibrator lay there for all to see.

"Here, let me help you." He went for the vibrator. Her face flushed when he held it up. It was hot pink and cracked down the middle. "It's broken."

Janie grabbed it from him and pushed the switch. It was jammed, stuck permanently in the "OFF" position. She shoved it in her purse and jumped up to leave. "I've got to go."

He calmly turned his hefty frame toward her. "Lady, you're not going to find another one."

The truth of his words was harsher than his face. Without a vibra-tor she couldn't participate in World Masturbation Day. She didn't know how to masturbate without it. And she hadn't had an orgasm in a year.

The rotund man slid off the chair. "I know a place that has vibrators. It's a secret, but I can take you there."

Janie was desperate. "Let's go."

"Later today we will talk to scientists who say that people who participate in World Masturbation Day may live longer. I'm Wolf Blitzer and I'll be shooting a load off with the rest of the world tomorrow."

*   *   *

The fat man led Janie out of the bar and down a narrow alleyway. "I'm Rush." He was breathing heavily from just a minute of walking.

"I'm Janie. Where are we going?" They turned down an isolated alley and her murder fears kicked in. He was so fat she knew she

could outrun him, but he could be hiding a number of weapons in those flesh flaps.

"Right here, actually." He stopped in front of a door marked NO ENTRY. He was about to knock but hesitated. "You might not like what you see."

She nodded. She hadn't liked what she'd seen since he sat down.

He knocked, and an attractive woman in her sixties opened the door. The woman glared at Rush and Janie through frameless glasses. Her hair cascaded around her shoulders like sleeping squirrels, and she smelled of wet fur and dried blood. Her face triggered an old memory.

"Oh my God, you're Sarah Palin." Janie was stunned.

The former vice-presidential candidate ignored her. "Rush, I told you it's over!"

The grotesque man flinched instinctively. "I think I might have left my pills here."

Palin looked Janie up and down. "Fine. But hurry, it's almost midnight."

Janie stumbled behind Rush into a dimly lit warehouse. She was still reeling from being in the presence of the aging maverick. Once the star of the Republican Party, Palin had faded into public obscurity in the last ten years. After a photo of her posing nude with a semiautomatic standing on top of a decapitated polar bear failed to make it into the NRA's 2017 calendar, she seemed to give up. But now she stood fiercely in front of the biggest tower of vibrators Janie had ever seen. The rainbow-colored hive was forty feet high and buzzing with fresh battery power. Sarah guarded the stash like a lioness.

"Go on and get your pills, Rush. You might have left them by those vibrating eggs." Rush darted out of sight, leaving Janie and Palin alone.

Janie's mind raced to think of what acceptable small talk she could offer. "I like your lipstick."

"Thank you, it's called 'Pitbull Gingivitis.' It's a new line that I created. Tested on animals and real Americans." Sarah's eyes bored into her skull. "You a real American?"

"Um, I think so." She wasn't even sure what that meant, especially coming from a woman hoarding a warehouse full of dildos. "May I buy one of these vibrators?"

Palin's eyes narrowed. "For what? World Masturbation Day? That's socialism at its worst. Big government does not tell me or anyone else to twiddle my twat!"

Janie couldn't believe what she was hearing. This unhappy blast from the past was squelching her future orgasm. "But I need one."

Palin let out a cackle that could recrack the Liberty Bell. "Well, you'll have to make a diddle wand out of wouldas and shouldas, because I own them all . . . and they are not for sale!"

Rush wheezed over with a box of vibrators. "Sarah, I couldn't find my pills. I'm just going to have to take these as compensation."

The faded beauty queen knocked the box out of his hands. "No one takes a single devil stick out of here!"

An errant vibrator rolled near Janie's feet. It was her chance. She grabbed the treasure and made a mad dash for the door. But just as her hand touched the knob, a bullet shattered a hole in the wall inches from her head. The ringing in Janie's ears from the gun harmonized with the steady hum of the vibrators.

"Sarah! Don't!" A large wet spot was growing on Rush's crotch.

"Shut up, Rush. Your girlfriend's a thief. Put the vibrator down." Janie started to set the vibrator down on the floor.

"No! On the pile." As Janie walked over to the pile, Palin followed her with the gun.

"Good girl. Now take these matches and light it for me. And then you can go." The gunslinger held out a pack of matches.

The thought of destroying hundreds of perfectly good orgasm machines made Janie sick. Another shot rang through the warehouse. "Do it!" Sarah seethed.

Janie hastily lit the matches and threw them onto the pile. The flames transformed the vibrators into the sexiest bonfire there ever was or will ever be. The smoke alarm went off and so did Palin's wristwatch.

Sarah ♡ Todd Sarah

"It's midnight, everyone! I've officially ruined World Masturbation Day for a good percentage of un-American women. Everyone get out! This place is becoming a death panel!"

The three stumbled outside into fresh air.

"Janie, I'm so sorry. I tried."

Janie took in the sad, pee-soaked man. All she wanted was to get the hell out of there. She turned to go.

"Wait! Before you leave, if I can just give you some advice . . . use your fingers. I know it takes longer than you want, but it's a bigger payoff than the vibrator. Just massage in a circle with these two fingers. I do it . . . because my penis is just that small."

Palin came up behind Rush. "Come on, Rush, I've got some news to broadcast on your radio show." A beaten Rush followed Palin into the night.

The festivities were already under way. People had stopped whatever they were doing and were relaxing on sidewalks, in bars, on top of cars, just taking care of their business in the street light. The warehouse fire was reflecting a warm orange glow off all the blissful faces. Firemen in mid-rescue had laid down the water hose for their own hose. Men and women were pleasuring themselves everywhere Janie looked. She was miserable. She ran to her apartment and locked the door.

She needed a vibrator. She was one of those women who never masturbated. It just wasn't in her. Outside people were moaning and laughing, tempting Janie to join. She got undressed.

She slowly slid her hand across her breast. She felt weird. She forced the feeling back and moved her other hand to her crotch. She squeezed it. It felt like a hairy coin purse. She pulled it open. Her hands were too cold. She rubbed them together and tried again. She slid her middle finger into the slot and wagged it around, like a spastic worm. It wasn't right.

"Just massage in a circle with these two fingers." Rush's words flashed in her head.

She found her clitoris and held it between her index finger and thumb. It felt like a small bean. She rubbed it slowly, and it started to tingle.

She rolled it clockwise and reverse, pressed it against her pelvic bone, and rubbed it against her labia. An excitement was spreading from her center through her thighs and into her arms. Her hand started moving on its own. Like it always knew what to do.

She had never felt this good in her entire life. **The few times that she was with a man she couldn't orgasm. And the one time with a vibrator it came on so fast and intense it was over in a metallic second.** But this was really building. She was topping her pleasure with every passing minute. Her hand was moving faster and faster. A loud moan escaped her lips, surprising her. She was on the precipice of an earth-shattering orgasm. Her eyes closed as every nerve ending in her vagina fanned out to squeeze liquid pleasure from her muscles and pour it through her body in wave after wave.

"I'm coming!" She screamed.

"So are we!" strangers screamed back.

She opened her eyes to a new reality. Janie had just rocked her own world all by herself. A huge smile spread across her face.

"It's World Masturbation Day, Sarah Palin. Go fuck yourself."

CHAPTER 5

Regular Sex:
The Straight and Narrow

Regular Sex:
The Straight and Narrow

Like eating your favorite food for every meal, having sex with the same person over and over quickly goes from boring to downright nauseating. It's enough to put you off "food" forever.

But it doesn't have to be that way.

*Marriage is the **fabric of society** (specifically cheesecloth, given that it rips half of the time).*

Just as a dash of paprika adds an unexpected kick to a glass of tap water, there are ways to spice up even the stalest crouton of a relationship. Sure, it's not as satisfying as sampling a different cuisine, but if you have any experience at the sexual buffet you know that sometimes "side dishes" don't exactly agree with the main course. And if one of those side dishes turns out to be crazy bread, it may just be your last meal.

In other words, love means making the best of your crouton. Which is why this chapter contains a million different ways to gussy up that pigeon food so you can keep forcing it down your gullet. Hey, at least you're not starving.

Now slather some lube on that ball and chain and make the best of it!

Make Your Bedroom a "Slow Zone"

One of the biggest mistakes couples make is letting the hustle and bustle of modern life interfere with their sex lives. Fax machines, VCRs, and Ataris all distract from taking the time your partner needs to feel appreciated. That's why we recommend making your bedroom a Slow Zone. That means no clocks, no responsibilities, no *anything* that takes away from dedicating yourself to satisfying your lover's needs, which, as you will soon discover, takes longer and longer the more they get sick of you.

CUDDLING

Cuddling, which goes by such other stomach-turning aliases as *snuggies, wuggies, snookie-wookies,* and *visits from Mr. Cozy Bear,* is an affirmation that the sexual experience you're about to share isn't just physical, it's emotional. Why else would you waste time locked in what basically amounts to a horizontal airport greeting when you could be doing something you actually enjoy? Because *you care,* that's why. In short, cuddling is a nonverbal way of telling your partner, "Hey, I'm not raping you." The sentiment will be appreciated.

FOREPLAY

After what will no doubt seem like hours of cuddling, you'll be ready to move on to the next phase of not having sex yet: foreplay. Put simply, foreplay is an attempt to compensate for the fact your mate is no longer excited by the mere sight of you. If you want to have intercourse, you're going to have to coax, beg, and otherwise trick your lover's genitals into engorging and/or moistening. It won't be easy.

Though other sexperts have dedicated entire books to arousal techniques and strategies, the best foreplay is achieved by simply listening to what your partner wants and then doing it, no questions asked. If it helps, make a checklist of all the things you have to do, then painstakingly go through the list item by item. Keep reminding yourself that it's fore*play*, not fore*work*, but try to avoid saying it out loud.

LOCKS ON THE DOOR

When all else fails, nothing prolongs a lovemaking session like a good, sturdy padlock. Or several padlocks. In fact, you might as well fortify that shit like a zombie attack is coming because once your partner gets off, it'll be the only thing stopping them from bolting into the next room. If you're clever, you'll hide the key in one of your erogenous zones. That'll get 'em back in bed!

be a bad girl!

Is there any truth to the rumor that crazy girls are more fun in bed? There's only one way to find out: get your psycho insane freak on! A relationship can only become interesting when it's unpredictable and dramatic. So pull down that halter top and unpack those daddy issues, it's time to take your man for a wild ride.

Follow these twelve taboo steps that will have him too scared to say no:

STEP 1: SURPRISE HIM!

Men loved to be surprised, especially if it's his penis being surprised by a warm mouth under his desk in the middle of work. Sneak out of bed at 3 am and hide in his office until it's time to make your move. Even if his satisfied moans get him fired, you'll still be inducted into the Bad Girl Hall of Fame.

STEP TWO: SCARE HIM

A good scare gets the heart racing, and that means the blood is getting to his penis even faster. Mug him in the parking lot. Wear a mask and carry a gun and ask for all his money. Then order him to give you all his penis money. If he's confused, make him dance by shooting bullets at his feet just as a bad girl does. Then have your way with him in the car. After he realizes that it was you all along he will be scared of you, but more important, he'll respect you.

STEP 3: PEE ON HIM

This is a great way to tell him you've lost control of your mind and your bladder. While you're doing it, be sure to look him directly in the eye so he knows that you know that the toilet is only a few feet away and you don't even care.

STEP FOUR: CUT YOURSELF

Tell your man that you're upset you haven't fused your spirits together with a blood ritual the way your parents did when they were young. Slice each other's palms with your trusty switchblade, then drink each other's blood. If he still isn't turned on, whip up a batch of blood margaritas. When you are done making love, say that cuddling is boring and carve his name into his chest. Every time he looks in the mirror he will remember who he is and that he has a real spark plug for a girlfriend.

STEP 5: MAKE UP A ~~SWEAR~~ WORD

Everyone says "fuck." It's become almost as inoffensive as the word "celery." But if you make up a word, like burtcod, and tell him that it means to fuck hard all night long, then you have a secret code between the two of you that is filthy dirty. And nothing's more enjoyable than talking like a sailor in front of Grandma with your very own foreign tongue. "Pass the asparagus, Grandma, I need all the energy I can get tonight to burtcod."

STEP 6:
Get Symbiotic Tattoos

Having strange men doodle on you like a used cocktail napkin has become passé as a form of rebellion. A real bad girl gets a tattoo on her genitals! Make your danger ditch look like a monkey; then, while he's sleeping, tattoo a banana on his penis. Once you both get over your skin infections, you can be sure your monkey will never go hungry!

Step 7: PUNCH HIS EX IN THE FACE

Or someone who looks like her. This will excite him because it might be something that he wanted to do but couldn't, until he found a bad girl like you. Occasionally, when you are out and about with him punch a stranger in the face. If he asks why you did that (he probably will), just say, "I thought that was your ex, and I wanted to punch her in the face."

STEP 8: **POOP** ON HIM

Just when he thought that it couldn't get any kinkier than you peeing on him, poop on him. Once you squat over him and lay your hot feces on his disbelieving chest he will have 'zero doubts that you are a completely crazy girl, and he'll have the physical evidence to prove it.

STEP 9: GET THROWN IN JAIL TOGETHER

Tired of having sex in the bedroom every night? Do something that gets you both arrested, like using his credit card to give money to Al-Qaeda. There's a good chance they'll put you in separate jail cells, but he'll have a shank in his pants imagining what kind of trouble you're getting into with the other bad girls.

Step 10: **SHAVE OFF ALL YOUR HAIR**

Being naughty requires a close shave down below. It's sexy to have him shave it for you, using whatever dirty razor or rusty vegetable peeler you can find. Then tell him that you want him to shave your head too. Only a bad girl wouldn't care about the classic aesthetics of feminine beauty. Then, when he's not looking, take all the hair (including the pubes) and send it to his mom. With no explanation!

Step 11: Tie Him Up

Taking control in the bedroom is a great way to show how wild you are. So try taking all the control. Tie him up. For days. Have your way with him and only feed him when he's loud. You'll be amazed how sexy and powerful you feel when only you have access to drinking water.

Step 12: Strip for Him

Teasing him with his own private peep show will make him fall in love with you all over again. Add some intricate dance moves that include jazz hands and pelvic gyrations. Put some modern dance in there to show him that you are passionate and artistic. Then just when he's worked into a frenzy, pee on him. Then poop on him. Then cut him. It will be a strip show he'll never forget. And he won't be able to get that kind of entertainment at any other club!

Take a "Role" in the Hay!

A surefire way to jazz up your sex life is by tricking your genitals into thinking they're with someone else. This is called **role-playing**.

The most important thing when role-playing is committing to the characters. If you're bashful about adopting sexy new identities, start by using each other's middle names. Don't you dare say you can't act—you've been faking genuine affection for years. Let go of your inhibitions the way you let go of your dreams! Before long, both of you will be acting up a sex storm. The characters may be pretend, but the orgasms will be as real as they come.

THE BONE IDENTITY

SETTING: A hotel room that looks similar to your bedroom.

CHARACTERS: Tatiana Glockenspecktor, a sexy assassin who has lured her target into a hotel room; **James Hamiltone,** a spy who has been smuggling hot secrets to the Russians for decades.

PROPS: Two pistols (preferably real).

COSTUMES: Tatiana should be wearing a trench coat with a rubber teddy underneath. James is dressed in a trench coat and tear-away three-piece suit.

OPENING DIALOGUE:

TATIANA: Thanks for meeting me here.

JAMES: It's hard to say no when there's a gun to your chest and cabbage breath in your face.

TATIANA: I apologize, I am German. I crave the sauerkraut.

JAMES: What else do you crave?

TATIANA, *pulling out gun:* You in a body bag. Which is the only thing you deserve for selling secrets to the Russians.

JAMES, *pulling out gun:* Well, I did keep one secret from them.

TATIANA: What?

JAMES: This!

James whips off his trench coat and tear-away three-piece suit revealing himself to Tatiana.

TATIANA: Oh my. That's a mighty big secret. We better hide it.

JAMES: I bet I know the perfect hiding place.

Tatiana takes off her trench coat and rubber teddy. Ad lib lovemaking.

UDDERLY SATISFIED

SETTING: A barn that looks a lot like your bedroom.

CHARACTERS: Marge Bickelworth, a prairie woman who is an incredibly talented cook; **Fred Bickelworth**, a man of the earth who has won several blue ribbons for his squash harvest.

PROPS: Pitchforks; one dairy cow.

COSTUMES: Both should be dressed in gingham shirts and overalls with removable crotch panel.

OPENING DIALOGUE:

FRED: Thank you for the grits this mornin', Margie. They made me feel like a new man.

MARGE: You're welcome, Fred. I love cookin' you grits.

FRED: I wish Bessie felt as good as me. Her teats are still dry today.

MARGE: I wonder what's gotten Bessie down lately.

FRED: I don't know. Here, squeeze her teat, maybe a woman's touch will help.

Marge squeezes Bessie's teat. Milk may or may not come out depending on whether the cow is calving. There are two alternate courses to take depending on the outcome.

IF MILK COMES OUT:

MARGE: She doesn't seem dry to me.

FRED: You must have magic hands. Maybe you can squeeze some milk out of this teat!

Fred rips off tear-away crotch panel.

MARGE: You have my favorite milk: condensed and sweet. It's just the ingredient I need for this love pie I'm cooking up.

Marge works Fred's "teat" and lovemaking transpires.

IF MILK DOES NOT COME OUT:

MARGE: Nothing's coming out.

FRED: Maybe you're doing it wrong.

MARGE: I need to be taught!

FRED: Come here, I'll teach you on my man-teat!

Fred rips off tear-away crotch panel and Marge proceeds to give him a teat job.

SWEATY YETI

SETTING: A mountainside in Nepal, or your kitchen with the refrigerator door open.

CHARACTERS: Yeti, a mythical creature often confused with her Bigfoot brother; **Daschel Scarsdale**, an ambitious cryptozoologist who has been searching for Bigfoot his whole life.

PROPS: A boulder; a small dead dog; a flash camera.

COSTUMES: Yeti is covered head to toe in fur. She also has a tear-away fur crotch covering. Daschel wears traditional khaki safari gear, with tear-away crotch.

OPENING DIALOGUE:

Yeti is hiding behind a boulder. Daschel has just discovered her.

DASCHEL: Heavens to Betsy! It's you! The one I've been searching for!

YETI: Hhhrrrrgh!

Yeti is frightened and cowers behind the boulder.

DASCHEL: Oh, please! Don't be scared, I'm your friend. Look, I brought your favorite food, small dog.

YETI: Whhhrrrrr!!

Yeti grabs the animal corpse and almost swallows it whole. She is starving.

DASCHEL: You like that. I knew you would. Finally the science world will accept me! Hold still for the camera, dear Bigfoot!

As Yeti swallows her last dog bone, Daschel aims his camera and flashes a shot. Yeti attacks him.

YETI: Aaaaaaarrrrhhggaah!

DASCHEL: Please, no, I'm sorry!

Yeti has Daschel pinned to the ground. They pause in their struggle to look into each other's eyes.

DASCHEL: Dear Bigfoot, you are the most beautiful creature my eyes have ever seen. Your magnificence has surpassed my dreams of you.

Daschel is so overwhelmed he cries uncontrollably. Yeti becomes filled with an animalistic sympathy. She instinctively rubs her whole body methodically against him.

YETI: Bbbbrrrrrrsch.

DASCHEL: This is so unexpected, this nurturing, it's so sensual. I have always been curious what the reproductive organs of a Bigfoot might feel like.

YETI: Jarjarjarjar!

Without warning Yeti rips off both her tear-away crotch and Daschel's and begins to yeti his brains out.

Just the Tip!

If your dying relationship has numbed you to the core, try anal sex. At least you'll feel something.

JOKES

YOU CAN PLAY IN BED

HUBBY ASLEEP BEFORE HIS HEAD HITS THE PILLOW? DOES YOUR OLD LADY GET MORE HEADACHES THAN A WOODPECKER IN A FLAGPOLE FACTORY? MAKE BEDTIME A GAS WITH *"SPANKY'S EROTIC NOVELTIES."*

CLIT BUZZER

BZZZZT!

Make touching your love button a hair-raising experience. The slightest pressure activates the gag and leaves 'em twitching. Great for first dates and trips to the gynecologist.
No. 2475............................. **$4.99**

EXPLODING PENIS It looks real, but give it a tug and it explodes with a loud **BANG.** Practically harmless.
No. 3443
Box of ten (not mailable)................**$9.99**

TOXIC SHOCKER Capsule filled with red liquid makes any time "that time of the month." Teach squeamish suitors a lesson they won't soon forget! Also works on husbands.
No. 1172........................... **$2.99**

FLY in the JIZZ!

FLY IN THE JIZZ Self-explanatory. An oldie but a goodie.
No. 946.........................
ONLY $**1**.99

HA HA HA

QUEEF CUSHION Faithfully re-creates that sound every gal knows and dreads. One hundred percent rubber for maximum volume and resonance.
No. 1005.................................... **$3.49**

FAKE PREGNANCY TESTER Keep the fun coming long after the deed is done. No matter how much she urinates on the stick, the results are inconclusive. A guaranteed laff-getter.
No. 7321
Box of one dozen............. **$5.99**

10 DAY FREE EXAMINATION MONEY BACK GUARANTEE

SPANKY'S EROTIC NOVELTIES, Dept. KR69 P.O. Box 69, New York, N.Y. 10022
I enclose $_____ (including 50¢ for postage and handling) as payment in full.

ITEM	QUANTITY	PRICE	ITEM	QUANTITY	PRICE
	TOTAL	$			

PRINT NAME_____

ADDRESS_____

CITY_____ STATE_____ ZIP_____

BE A good guy!

» IS IT TRUE THAT CHICKS LOVE THE SWEETEST OF DICKS? WIPE THAT MAPLE SYRUP OFF YOUR SCHLONG AND FIND OUT THE HARD WAY: BY BEING NICE! FOLLOW THESE EIGHT SIMPLE TIPS, AND BEFORE LONG, YOU'LL BE CATCHING SEX FLIES WITH SPOONFULS OF GENTLEMAN HONEY.

COMPLIMENT HER FACE » Tell her she's pretty, but really go into detail. Say her eyes sparkle like chrome on a Corvette and her nose looks a bitchin' hood ornament. If you run out of things to say, compare her to a beautiful horse. Chicks love horses.

MAKE HER DINNER IN BED » A woman's taste buds are never more sensitive than when they're tasting things in bed. Prepare her an elegant meal that she has to digest horizontally and be prepared for a hot roll in the crumbs! If you want to keep getting that kind of action, keep her bedridden by serving her breakfast, lunch, and intravenous midnight snacks. After a while, she'll be immobilized due to atrophy, but those stomach and vagina muscles will be in tip-top shape!

GIVE HER ALL YOUR MONEY » You could buy your girl any number of things that would make her happy: diamonds, designer gowns, babies. But in the end you are just going to give her all your money. So why not get it out of the way? Write her a check, or just sign your bank account over to her. Now you've just bought your lady the best present of all, the security of knowing you are financially unable to leave her.

BE HER PERSONAL DOORMAN » If you're a nice guy, your lady shouldn't have to open a door ever again (and she may not be able to, if you've been properly bed-feeding her!). Open doors until she starts taking it for granted. Then, pretend your arms are broken. When she can't leave the room, she'll realize you're the guardian angel who's been turning all those knobs, and will reward you by polishing yours.

RUB HER FEET » The way to a woman's heart isn't through her ear holes or even her vagina–it's through her feet! On the bottom of the foot are nerve endings and pressure points connected to every single organ in the body. So take advantage of them! Think her breasts could be a little bigger? Work those feet, son! You can awaken nerves in the feet connected to the boobs that will activate them. And she won't have any idea what your true motive is. All she'll know is that you are a great guy who rubs her feet for four hours every night.

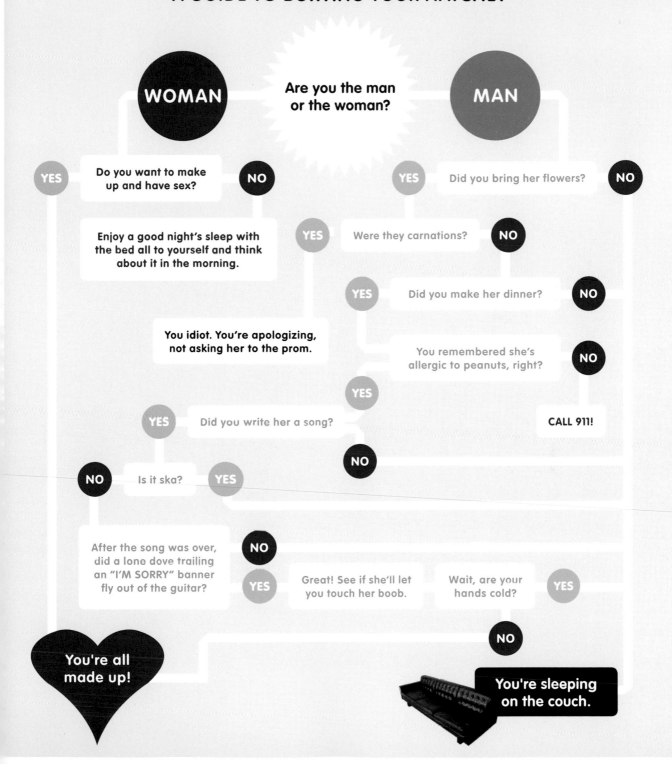

Centerfold Data Sheet

Name: The Sexy Book of Sexy Sex

Bust: 17"

Waist: 17"

Hips: 17"

Weight: 1.55 lbs

Birth date: August 15th, 2010

Birthplace: San Francisco, CA

Ambitions: To get on OPRAH

Turn-ons: Encyclopedias, almanacs, Kindles

Turn-offs: Dirty hands, Itty Bitty book lights

Worst Job: Propping up a wobbly table leg at Shoney's

Most Embarrassing Moment: Coming back from the printer and realizing I'd forgotten my dust jacket!

Hobbies: Water sports

Ugly Duckling Photo:

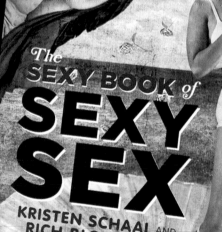

The SEXY BOOK of
SEXY SEX

KRISTEN SCHAAL AND
RICH BLOMQUIST

WITH ILLUSTRATIONS BY MICHAEL KUPPERMAN
AND LISA HANAWALT

Sand Whispers

Welcome to SandWhispers™, the world's premier erotic destination. Whether you're celebrating a new love or rekindling the flames of passion, the SandWhispers Sexperience™ is guaranteed to pamper, tempt, and titillate you and your love-mate to new heights of ecstasy. At SandWhispers, there are no limits to how sexy you can be!*

Skindinavia

Some of the most beautiful people in the world are Scandinavian . . . you! Take the Fondela Gondola to SandWhispers' Viking-themed love nook of the North. Get cozy at night to avoid freezing to death, and come morning, you'll be ready to rape and pillage . . . each other!

GRÜNDELBEACH: Forget nude beaches, Skindinavia is home to the world's only nude fjord. Take a super-quick skinny dip and become a member of the SandWhispers Polar Bare Club.

ICE MOTEL: Hourly rates make this the perfect place for a secret rendezvous. But don't get too hot and bothered . . . your room might melt!

THE MATTERHORNY: Let our sex sherpas guide you to the peak of ecstasy. Then, hit the slopes on one of our covered Love Toboggans for a private getaway all the way down the mountain.

Plymouth Cock EROTIC COLONIAL VILLAGE

Step back in time and experience romance as a settler in the New World. Let your passions be as untamed as the wilderness—Plymouth Cock is anything but puritanical.

YE OLDE CANDLE SHOPPE: Dip your wick in history as you help Lazarus the blind candlestick maker beef up his inventory. Be careful with the hot wax . . . but not too careful!

HESTER'S WIG PARLOR: Look the part with an authentic colonial merkin. Our wigmakers will fashion a stylish powdered wig to conceal your modern muff.

GENITAL STOCKADE: In Plymouth Cock they don't hand out scarlet letters. Get in trouble with the law and you'll endure pubic humiliation with your private parts on display in the town square.

CHIEF HUMPING HORSE'S SURPRISE ATTACK: Every hour on the hour, the horniest tribe this side of the Mississippi launches a savage panty raid on the colony. Protect your britches, my lord!

THE LOST CITY OF SEXLANTIS

Your love will never be deeper than it is in Sexlantis, SandWhispers' legendary underwater kingdom. There's no better place to come out of your shell!

ORAL REEF: Explore the ins and outs of this fragile undersea habitat and give your special lady a pearl necklace.

SEAHORSEBACK RIDING: A classic romantic pastime with an underwater twist. Don't be afraid to go bareback!

BLUE-LIGHT DISTRICT: Always wondered how mermen get it on? Enjoy a delicious seafood dinner while being educated by a mermaid sexcapade.

WHALE WATCH STRIPTEASE: Let your excitement and patience build as you remove one item of clothing with every sighting. It could be days!

STUDI⊙69

Lights . . . camera . . . romance! The glitz and glamour of Tinseltown get a sexy makeover at SandWhispers' very own movie studio. At Studio 69, your love is the star!

CREAMWORKS: Make a sex tape with high production values with the help of a real Hollywood crew. At Creamworks, the nudity is always tasteful.

SEXY DOUBLE DARE: Shimmy through slime and tumble through tapioca as you and your lover compete in this erotic

update of the yuckiest game show on television. Your public displays of affection just got even grosser!

PRIXAR: Too shy to make a sex tape? Jump into a pair of motion-capture suits and let Studio 69's animators turn you into a naughty cartoon. Get ready to be rendered in 3-D: Dangerous, Doable, and Deviant.

WALK OF FAME: Press your naked bodies into the wet cement and become part of Studio history. But watch out for paparazzi!

¡TOGA LOCO!
Latin meets Latin in Toga Loco, where hot-blooded Hispanic passion mingles with the grandeur of Ancient Rome. It's two sexy themes in one!

TROJAN PIÑATA: Strap on your blindfolds and get swinging . . . what's inside will ambush you with sexiness!

CASA DEL BATH: Steam your cares away in a real Roman bath while being serenaded by a waterproof mariachi band.

EMPEROR FROG'S: Rome is burning! Or is it that the picante sauce? Either way, two-for-one tequila shooters and a working vomitorium are a match made on Mount Olympus. All hail Emperor Frog!

SandWhispers is a traditional couples-only resort.

LEGEND

 Coed Restrooms   Additional Porking

 Nude Court   Sinformation Booth

The Mile High Club

Rex and Stacee boarded the plane sexily, their loins still aching from a lust-filled week at SandWhispers, the world's premier adult fantasy resort. For the past seven days the newlyweds had experienced every sexual fantasy they could conceive of, and a few SandWhispers' team of Love Engineers had invented especially for them. The aging stewardess greeted the lovers with a knowing smile. She saw a lot of oversexed couples limping their way back from SandWhispers with stars in their eyes and ice on their crotches. But something about these two was different. They must have *really* fucked each other's brains out.

Rex regular-smiled back at the stewardess. As he made his way down the aisle, his eyes zeroed in on his bride's shapely apple bottom. He wondered what kind of apple his love's derriere most resembled and finally settled on Macoun. Firm yet juicy, and excellent in a salad. Rex felt his prick stiffen in his Jams, which he'd purchased for SandWhispers' Sexy Eighties theme brunch. Of all the sex-meals they'd savored in the past week, it may have been Rex's favorite. They never did find Stacee's leg warmers.

Stacee opened the overhead compartment and hoisted up her suitcase. Rex saw his chance. He sidled up behind his bride and pressed his taut manhood into her pillowy rump.

"Rex!" Stacee scolded. "Put that thing away before you get Tasered by the air marshal!"

"Let him try," Rex cooed. "I've got him outgunned."

The lovebirds settled into their seats and Rex covered his Jams bulge with a SkyMall catalog. After seven days of submitting to their every carnal desire, the next four hours weren't going to be easy. It added up to literally hundreds of miles of nonstop celibacy. As the stewardess went through the motions of the safety demonstration, Rex slid his hand under Stacee's ample fanny.

"Didn't you get enough this week?" Stacee giggled. "Or should I have given you two blow jobs when we were parasailing?"

"Sorry, baby, I can't help myself. I saw you reaching up to adjust that little air nozzle and it made me think of what we did at SandWhispers' Erotic Colonial Village."

"You mean with the bellows?" Stacee grinned. "The ones we 'borrowed' from the blacksmith?"

"Yeah . . ." Rex could still feel the musty air tickling the tip of his erect penis, freshly drizzled with hot beeswax. Rex had read enough history to know SandWhispers had taken some license with their overtly sexual applications of colonial-era technology, but he wasn't complaining.

"I can't wait to use that scrimshaw vibrator we bought at the gift shop," Stacee said, nervously patting the outside pocket of her carry-on. "Do you think we'll have any trouble getting it through customs?"

"I doubt it. It's not real whalebone."

Finally the plane lifted off the runway. The couple watched as their sexual playground faded into the distance like the last spots of butterscotch on Rex and Stacee's body sundaes. Now the only topping on Rex's skin was beads of blue-ball sweat. He wasn't going to make it. Somehow, his blood-starved brain hatched a plan.

"Hey Stacee, I've got an idea. We should go to the bathroom."

"Good idea. Before the beverage cart blocks the aisle."

"No," Rex said, caressing her upper arm. "We should both go . . . together."

"You mean . . . join the Mile High Club?!" Stacee's face flushed. "You can't be serious."

"Serious as a fart attack," Rex said, misremembering an expression he'd heard on TV. "I need you."

Stacee's heart raced. Was she really thinking about doing it in an airplane bathroom? It would be her riskiest sexcapade to date, even more daring than the time she masturbated in the dressing rooms at Gap, Banana Republic, and Old Navy all in the same day. Still, the idea intrigued her. "What if someone knocks on the door when we're in there?" she asked, remembering a close call at Abercrombie.

Rex thought for a second. "I'll say you're diabetic and I was giving you your shot. They need shots and shit, right?"

"What if they ask to see the needle?"

"Shit, you're right." Rex's mind raced faster than the blood to his penis. "Ooh, I know! I could say I was holding your hair back while you puked."

"You're a genius." Stacee grabbed her husband by the back of the neck and kissed him hard.

Without another word, Stacee got up and made her way to the bathroom. She stared straight ahead, avoiding eye contact with anyone for fear she'd already switched to her bedroom eyes. Stacee had nearly reached the restroom when a wobbly old Frenchman emerged. He held open the door and flashed an apologetic smile. "Thair ees no twalett papair een thair."

Stacee was so focused on being inconspicuous that she answered without thinking. "That's perfect, thank you."

The Frenchman gave her a puzzled look and returned to his seat, glancing back at her the whole way.

Stacee was tempted to call the whole thing off. But then she saw Rex licking his lips, daring her to be a bad girl. It was maybe the hottest thing Stacee had ever seen. Emboldened, she took a deep breath and closed herself inside the bathroom.

The bathroom was barely big enough for one person, let alone two. Stacee took a good look at herself in the mirror. She was pretty. If she pouted her lips and squinted her eyes, she was even sexy. If she flipped her dress over her face and opened her legs, she was a sex object. She took off her sweater and wedged it in the paper towel dispenser. It almost felt like a dressing room. And when Rex knocked on the door she felt dangerous.

Stacee pulled open the door a few inches and wedged herself by the toilet so that Rex could squeeze through. He entered, erection first. Rex closed the door behind him and locked it.

"Jesus. How did you get that thing down the aisle?" she whispered, instinctively grabbing it and peeling down his Jams like they were a splotchy, fluorescent banana peel.

"Jedi mind trick. Now take this skyfucker's light saber, my princess."

Stacee steadied herself against both walls of the bathroom while lifting her leg onto the sink. Her foot came down on the soap dispenser, and blue gel squirted everywhere. Rex was having an equally hard time wrangling his rigid cock in such close quarters. He might as well have been trying to break a piñata inside a phone booth. Stacee's hip hit the flush button, and a mighty WHOOSH roared from the stainless-steel bowl.

"Just . . . try to get under . . . "

"I'm trying! I'm trying!"

"Are you in?"

"That's my elbow. Hold on."

Rex grabbed a handful of blue soap and smeared it on his forearm, hoping the extra lube would let him slide it up and over Stacee's knee. It worked. That accomplished, he went about the tricky business of guiding his shaft into her glistening triangle. In the cramped lavatory it was hard to miss . . . and it was waiting for him.

Stacee couldn't believe it. She was having sex in an airplane bathroom. Though the accomplished librarian spent her days surrounded by knowledge, nothing in those musty books could have prepared her for the ecstasy she experienced in that Newark-bound fuck-cubby. With each of Rex's powerful thrusts the bathroom shook. Was it turbulence, or was the jackhammer action of Rex's cock actually putting the plane in danger? Neither of them cared. Lust was at the controls now, and Pleasure was the copilot.

Rex and Stacee's simultaneous sky orgasm rivaled anything they had experienced at SandWhispers. When it was over they collapsed into each other's arms and panted like newborn colts, weak-kneed and in desperate need of a good brushing.

Suddenly, there was a knock on the door. Rex and Stacee froze.

"You all right in there?" It was the stewardess.

"What do we do?" Stacee whispered.

Rex's face took on a look of resolve. "We pull up our underwear and act cool."

Rex drew a deep breath and pushed open the door. There was a long line of people waiting to use the bathroom. It was exactly what Rex and Stacee had been afraid of. Stacee tugged on Rex's sleeve, silently signaling him to stick to the plan.

"My wife is diabetic so I was holding her hair!" Rex blurted.

They were busted.

The remaining three hours and forty minutes of the four-hour flight were understandably awkward. As a copilot, Pleasure had been nothing but accommodating to the couple's sexual needs, but the actual copilot was far less sympathetic. He told Rex and Stacee he could have them arrested and even made them clean up the soap in the bathroom while the other passengers watched. Fortunately for Rex and Stacee, he was used to dealing with amorous SandWhispers clientele and let them off easy. Still, the experience was mortifying. With a planeful of laughing eyes upon him, Rex couldn't have gotten another erection even if he wanted to. And he definitely didn't want to.

When they finally landed, the humbled newlyweds made their way to the baggage carousel to claim their suitcases full of SandWhispers erotic souvenirs. As Rex and Stacee waited for their bags they silently hoped none of the other passengers would approach them for one last indignity. But their luck had been lost along with their luggage. The old man from the flight shuffled their way, his mocking French cackle echoing through the baggage claim. As he drew closer, he ogled Rex and Stacee head to toe as though trying to conjure a better mental image of them in the act. "Eef eet eesn't zee leetle love-bairds," he sneered.

Rex tried yet again to make sense of his botched postcoital alibi. "Diabetes! I was holding her hair, er, I mean needle—"

Rex didn't have a chance to finish. The Frenchman pulled a canister from his coat and sprayed a fine purple mist in Rex's and Stacee's faces. The smell reminded Stacee of cupcakes and how nice it was to take a little nap after eating six or seven of them.

Then everything went black.

Stacee and Rex woke with a jolt. It felt like an earthquake.

"Oh, lovebairds! Are you awake, mon chéries?"

Stacee lifted the rosewater-infused cucumber slices from her eyes. Her head was throbbing, and she was having trouble focusing. "What the—?! Where are we?"

The Frenchman eased her back onto the massage table. "Eet's joost tairbulance."

It was only then that Stacee became aware of the gentle hum of an engine. They were on an airplane. And not just any airplane, but one with a beautifully tiled Russian spa and working steam room.

Their attacker had traded his rumpled travel clothes for a crisp butler's uniform and now presented them with a bottle of champagne. Rex, an ex-sommelier, read the label and gasped. "That's Louis Roederer, Cristal Brut 1962. It's $17,625 a bottle!"

The Frenchman just sniffed. "Eet ees compliments of zee president."

As if on cue, the oldest woman Rex and Stacee had ever seen made an entrance. She looked like a skeleton, the flowing white scarf around her neck seemingly the only thing keeping her head attached to her body. Despite this, she held herself with an air of superiority, taking a long drag off her cigarette holder before she spoke. When she did, the words came quick and urgent like a reporter in an old movie, staccato puffs of smoke punctuating each syllable.

"Stacee, Rex, sorry for the Shanghai treatment. My man was a little trigger-happy with that voodoo gas. Hope the fancy booze made up for the crop dusting. Allow me to introduce myself. I'm Amelia Earhart, Presidentrix for Life of the Mile High Club."

The words nearly blew Rex and Stacee out of their cashmere slippers. Could it be? Had they really been kidnapped by the shaggy-haired heroine of the skies, the woman who single-handedly took the cock out of cockpit, only to tragically put the Ms. in missing? Before Stacee could challenge their captor, Rex spoke for both of them.

"Bullshit. If you're Amelia Earhart, you'd be like two hundred years old!"

The scarved mistress ignored Rex and looked to Stacee. "Your hubby sure has a way with words. It's no wonder he talked you into bumping uglies in the bathroom."

Stacee felt as though she'd been slapped in the face. Having strangers know about her bathroom tryst was embarrassing enough. But hearing the famed aviatrix mention her skanky sky-romp was like having Susan B. Anthony walk in on her giving a blow job in a voting booth.

The Frenchman pussyfooted up to Earhart balancing an impossibly long-stemmed martini on his tray. Amelia plucked the glass off the tray and took a graceful sip. "This is Fred Noonan, my manservant and sometime navigator. I say 'sometime' because he certainly wasn't doing it over Howland Island."

The butler's whole body slumped, resigned to this sort of abuse. Stacee's brow furrowed. Something seemed fishy, and it wasn't the caviar hors d'oeuvres. "I thought Fred Noonan was from Illinois."

The butler gave a pained sigh. "She makes me talk like zis. Pardon mois while I breeng moir dreenks."

Amelia swigged down the rest of her towering martini and got back to business. "I suppose you two are wondering why you're here. You randy rabbits don't realize it, but when you made whoopee in that airplane bathroom, you joined an elite group."

Rex was confused. "Are you saying us fucking on the plane was a *good* thing?"

"Now you're on the trolley," Amelia laughed, giving Rex a congratulatory slap on the back. "Every bone in your body—well, almost every one—told you canoodling in the can was a bad idea, yet you two still did it. That takes real moxie. The stuff leaders are made of." Amelia pulled a jewelry box from her pocket and presented Rex and Stacee with what looked like pilot's wings. "Welcome to the Mile High Club."

"Your drinks." In a flash, Noonan had returned with two cocktails frothing out of matching penis pumps. Stacee recognized it instantly. Not twenty-four hours ago she had proclaimed the Foamy Cocksucker her new favorite drink while lounging poolside at the resort. "How . . . how did you know?"

"SandWhispers is just one of the many business ventures controlled by the Mile High Club," Amelia boasted.

"Pigs in a blanket?" Noonan offered the pampered abductees an even silverer tray of tiny hot dogs.

Rex downed the contents of his penis pump in a single gulp. "If you guys are such hot shit, what do you want from us? Are you looking for more flunkies or something? Because I don't play butler."

Noonan rolled his eyes at Rex's posturing. He'd seen this routine a thousand times, from men far more powerful. Heads of state. Captains of industry. Anyone who'd had the audacity to make love in an airplane lavatory. In the end, they always succumbed to Amelia's wishes.

"Cool your propellers, bub. You and little Miss Encyclopedia here are VIPs: Very Important Pals-of-Yours-Truly," Amelia said, jabbing her sternum with her bony thumb. "How 'bout I give you the dime tour?"

With that the spa door opened, revealing the main cabin of the plane. It was spectacular. Dozens of couples milled around a luxurious lounge, covered from floor to ceiling with red shag carpet. There was a gold Jacuzzi, a sushi and cocktail bar, a contortionist, and a trapeze artist. The room was lined with plush red couches almost invisible against the matching carpet, which were covered with couples cuddling. But what caught Stacee's eye more than anything were the two bathrooms bookending the bar. They were as small as the one they'd made love in, something Stacee could tell even from where she was standing because they were made of glass.

When Amelia walked into the room everyone went silent. "Hello, lovelies. I'd like you to meet the newest members of the Mile High Club, Rex and Stacee." The introduction was met with eerie silence. Stacee felt a familiar chill, something she hadn't felt since Abercrombie. It was fear. "What's with the silent treatment?" Amelia barked. "Did cats shit on your tongues? Say hello!"

Instantly and all at once, the club members muttered lukewarm greetings. Most of the couples were Rex and Stacee's age and were dressed casually, but a few old-timers were wearing threadbare vintage clothes. Stacee was having trouble taking it all in, especially since her bladder was pushing against her brain. "Is there a bathroom I can use?"

"There are two right by the bar, so you can wet your whistle on the way back. Rexy, maybe you'd like to join your better half for another roll in the soap?"

Rex and Stacee looked at each other in horror. For all the experimenting they did at SandWhispers, the thought of having sex in see-through bathrooms for a captive audience was something they never wanted to try.

"Actually, I was hoping that you had a more private bathroom?" Stacee surveyed the room but couldn't make out any doors on the shaggy walls.

"You're out of luck, toots. Those are the only two cans on the plane."

Stacee cursed her small bladder and the two exquisite drinks that filled it. "That's okay. I'll just wait till we get home."

This tickled Amelia pinker than the penis pump drinks, and her laugh boomed throughout the cabin.

"Ahhh, Stacee . . . Rex . . . My dear sweet horny treats. That's the thing about the Mile High Club. Once you're in, you're in for life. You're never going home."

"You can't be serious!" Rex protested.

Amelia looked him dead in the eye. "Serious as a heart attack."

"It's fart attack," Rex said, correcting her.

The muffled sobs of the other couples told Stacee and Rex she wasn't bluffing. They looked around and took in their new home. Then Stacee made her way to the bathroom. "I'm going to need another Foamy Cocksucker."

**Federated
Airline Agency**

LET THIS BE A LESSON

Having sexual intercourse in aircraft lavatories isn't just dangerous, it's ILLEGAL. Since the Underwear Bomber incident of Christmas 2009, the only two activities allowed in airplane bathrooms are urinating and defecating. Also, aircrafts have a limited supply of hand soap, and using excess amounts for sexual lubrication could lead to potentially unsanitary conditions. Although this is a cautionary tale using fictional characters, the Mile High Club is very real. It just goes by a different name: jail. If you absolutely must make love, please do it in your seat, trying your best not to disturb fellow passengers. TOGETHER WE CAN DEFEAT TERRORISM. Thank you.

A MESSAGE FROM THE FAA

CHAPTER 6

The Gay Chapter

The Gay Chapter

The **pink triangle** is an international symbol of gay pride. Originally used to identify homosexuals in Nazi concentration camps, the gay community made it their own by flipping it upside down. Take that, Hitler!

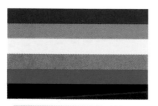

The **rainbow flag**, whose colors represent the diversity of the gay community. Take that, homophobic leprechauns!

Well hello, sailor. I'm the gay chapter. I couldn't help but notice you reading me. Don't be shy. We're all a little gay; some of us just happen to be a lot gay. And we all love tits no matter what. It's just a fact of life.

In a perfect world, homosexuality would be celebrated, not condemned. Two souls find each other in the vast sea of humanity and know exactly how to work each other's equipment: that's magic. If you weren't gay, you might even be a bit resentful. Oh wait, some people are! It's like they know we have more fun and they can't stand it.

Look, can we be real for a minute? Even back when I was still a first draft, I knew deep down inside that I was a gay chapter. Sure, I tried to hide it. I convinced myself it was just a phase and I'd be straight after the next rewrite. For a while, I even switched to the most conservative font I could find. (Courier . . . yuck!) But eventually, I realized I had to be honest with myself and do what made me happy. Pursuit of happiness? Sound familiar? It's in the Constitution. And if you think a straight man had handwriting that fancy, then you have a few things to learn about calligraphy.

FUCKTOID

Historians believe James Buchanan was our first gay president, though Abraham Lincoln is remembered as the one with the obvious beard.

President Buchanan was so distraught by the death of his fiancée he spent the rest of his life fucking men in the anus.

ESCAPE FROM THE CLOSET:

Tips on Coming Out

If we lived in a more tolerant time, coming out wouldn't be such a big deal. But until the self-righteous get that stick out of their fart holes (and then put it back in again in a nice rhythmic fashion), here are some suggestions for your gay rebranding.

COME OUT ONE BODY PART AT A TIME

Coming out cold turkey can be jarring to both you and your loved ones. So do it gradually! Start with a flaming gay pinky toe. Then try being light in only one loafer. Before you know it, everyone will be dying for that frumpy last straight hair to fall out so the party can really start.

FAKE YOUR DEATH

If you suspect your family would disown an openly gay you, nothing will fix them like a good death scare! It takes meticulous planning and a lot of money for the crashed hang glider next to the crocodile pit, but it's worth every penny to see the looks on their faces when you emerge alive and well at your own funeral. Only now you're gay! They'll be so happy to see you they'll leave their ignorance in the casket.

THE SECOND COMING

If the reason that you're scared to come out to your family is that Jesus told them being gay is a sin, then it's time for them to get another message from Jesus! With an old bedsheet, some thorns, and a lot of dramatic lighting you can help the Lord spread his message of loving your neighbor, even if that neighbor is a gaybor. Make sure you cast an out-of-town actor to play Christ, as it might be awkward for your parents to run into Jesus again at the supermarket.

ESCAPE FROM THE CLOSET:

WITNESS PROTECTION PROGRAM

If you want to avoid coming out to your friends and family completely, tell them you're going into the Witness Protection Program. Lie about some gangster murder you saw and say your good-byes. Let them know that if they do want to see you, you'll be living out your life in Key West, Florida, as a gay person! You don't know how you're going to pull it off (wink, wink), but at least you'll be safe.

THROW YOUR OWN PARADE

Get it out there, get it in their face, get it on a float! Everybody loves a parade, especially if there's a chance of catching some candy or beads. But they'll also be catching something else . . . the drift!

BECOME A CONSERVATIVE, FAMILY-VALUES REPUBLICAN

The family-values platform isn't just the antigay agenda this party endorses, it's also the name of the floating raft they want to put all gays onto and push out to sea. Yet everyone knows many (if not all) of these so-called defenders of "family values" are intolerant of gay people because they're compensating for the secret shame they feel about their own homosexual urges. Which is exactly why you should become one! That way, you can avoid discrimination while still planting the seed that you're probably gay. If you can't beat 'em, join 'em! Then, slip into the men's room at the country club and fuck 'em!

Fisting: A TRAINING GUIDE

Whether you and your partner have zero penises or an abundance of them, nothing brings variety to an orifice like a good, clenched fist. Popular in the gay community, fisting has crossed over to everyone. But before you go punching the pink, take a moment to bone up on the finer points of fisting. It requires patience, ambition, and a lot of practice. Here are some tips to get you ready for your first fisting.

FIND A PARTNER

No, you cannot fist yourself. Well, technically you can. But trust us: when you finally succeed and are sitting fist-deep on your arm, you will know what true loneliness is. And it will shake your soul.

PICK A HOLE

Determine right from the beginning who will be the fister and who will be the fistee. A good way to decide is by playing rock-paper-scissors. If one of you picks "rock," your training will have already begun!

WAS I WEARING A RING?

Before you get serious about finger spelunking, you'll want to remove any jewelry or press-on fingernails. Also make sure that Band-Aids are secure and warts are dormant. Mittens are probably a bad idea, no matter how cold it is.

K-WHY? BECAUSE YOU HAVE TO!

Just by looking you will notice that your hand is about seven times larger than your partner's vagina or anus. Put on a coat of lube armor. You're going to need it to battle the laws of physics.

SET A SCHEDULE

Don't expect to get full fistage on the first try. You'll need to set a rigorous training schedule with your partner. Hang a calendar in a prominent place as a reminder. If company comes over and asks why Monday, Wednesday, and Friday have a fist sketched on them, you can protect your privacy by telling them you've joined the Black Panther Party.

TAPERING OFF

Like any good marathoner, you need to rest up before the big event. When you've gotten everything in but your thumb, treat yourself to a few days off. Both of you need to recuperate, especially the one getting fisted. At this point, the only thing you should be cramming into your body is carbohydrates and a lot of water.

THE FINAL PUSH

After a week or two of training you'll be ready for the main event. Start slow like always: fingertips, then knuckles. Then take a deep breath and dive on in. When you're wrist-deep . . . STOP! "Arming" is only for professionals, and if you're Popeye you could kill someone.

Lesbian Bed Death

It happens every three minutes. A lesbian couple's sex life comes to a quiet end. But the real tragedy is that in most cases, the victims don't even notice.

This police report was obtained using the Freedom of Information Act.

SEXY SEX POLICE DEPARTMENT

INCIDENT REPORT *STATEMENT*

INCIDENT NO. | 9 | 0 | 0 | 2 | 2 | 7 | 0 | 6 | 9

LOCATION	DATE/TIME REPORTED:
PARK SLOPE, BROOKLYN	Wednesday 11:45:00

INCIDENT TYPE/OFFENSE:
1.) LESBIAN BED DEATH

REPORTING OFFICER	APPROVING OFFICER
GOODMAN, Casey	SCHWARTZ, Pepper

PERSONS

ROLE	NAME	SEX.	ADDRESS
WITNESS	Gladys Kravitz	F	XXXXXXXXXXX Brooklyn

OFFENDERS

DEFENDANT	Dani Reilly	F	XXXXXXXXXXX Brooklyn
DEFENDANT	Alex Parker	F	XXXXXXXXXXX Brooklyn

NARRATIVE

I responded to a call at 10:15 PM from Ms. Kravitz, who said she has been the suspects' neighbor for approximately three years. She stated that for the first two years after the couple moved in she could hear sexual noises about once a week through her wall. But in the past year she hasn't heard the noises at all and was worried.

page 1 of 2

I immediately headed to the residence. When I arrived I could hear season three of The L Word through the door. I knocked on the door and Alex Parker answered. I could tell by her behavior that it was unusual for anyone to visit the apartment. She yelled at her partner Dani Reilly to "push pause I gotta know if Shane goes through with it!" Reilly yelled back, "Of course she's going through with it!" And they went back and forth like this for a while before I was invited to enter.

I walked into the apartment and was instantly struck by the odor. It smelled of stale popcorn and zucchini bread. The couch had two distinct indentations where the suspects regularly sit. These indentations were exactly four feet apart. On the TV the actress Katherine Moennig was frozen, and below her were piles of DVDs. The suspects were dressed in sweatpants and flannels. I asked if this was their nightly attire and they confirmed it was their standard uniform in the home. I then asked to see the bedroom. Both parties seemed very nonchalant about revealing what should be an intimate room.

In the bedroom I saw a queen-sized bed neatly covered in a pastel quilt. On closer inspection of the quilt I saw that there was a discoloration towards the center, a stain of some sort. Hopeful, I inquired what it was. Parker said that a deceased dog had an accident several months ago. I asked if there were any other pets that shared the bed with them and they introduced me to a black Lab named Bette and a pit bull named Barney Frank. I was told that the pets had not spent a single night on the floor.

I then asked if they owned sex toys of any sort. It took several minutes for the suspects to remember if they had any in their possession. Parker thought there might be a vibrator in her nightstand drawer. I opened said drawer and saw a vibrator encased in a spider web.

After seeing this I investigated the bathroom. On the side of the bath I saw a lone pubic hair. I called each suspect individually into the bathroom and asked if they knew whether the pubic hair came from their partner or if they had shaved their pubic regions recently. Reilly laughed and said: "It's been months since any hair pie has been eaten around here."

It was then that I called for backup.

Casey Goodman
REPORTING OFFICER

Pepper Schwartz
APPROVING OFFICER

LET'S GAY

Does putting up with the closed-minded homophobia of your neighbors, clergy, or pets ever make you want to just get out of town? Well, do it! Just be careful where you go. As of 2009, homosexuality was illegal in seventy-eight countries. That means that unless your genitals have diplomatic immunity, you could be arrested, jailed, or even executed just for being gay. And you thought high school was bad.

To avoid run-ins with the law, use the following map when planning your next gaycation. Steer clear of countries whose tacky, homophobic plaid clashes with the stripes of the gay pride rainbow.

CALIFORNIA
Homosexuality not illegal but gay marriage banned since 2008. Children remain safely in the hands of unemployed, fame-hungry heterosexuals living with their parents.

JAMAICA
Hey mon! Don't even think of getting any "mon-on-mon" action here, where gay sex is punishable by ten year's hard labor. (Lesbian sex is legal, so long as it is performed for the sake of getting one's groove back.) Lack of gay meeting spots may explain the sudden popularity of bobsledding in 1980s.

GUYANA
The only South American nation where homosexuality is still illegal. Probably compensating for the fact that most people thought it was "a little gay" back when it was British Guiana.

BARBADOS
Homosexuality punishable by life in prison. Which would be okay, if prison was outside.

GAY LEGEND

≡ = Legal

▤ = Illegal

TWINKIE SCALE OF UNCONTROLLED HOMOPHOBIA
(as established in the Harvey Milk murder trial)

🏷 = Gay-friendly

🏷 🏷 = Gay-acquainted

🏷 🏷 🏷 = Don't ask, don't tell

🏷 🏷 🏷 🏷 = The claws are out

🏷 🏷 🏷 🏷 🏷 = Smear the queer

EGYPT

While not explicitly illegal, homosexuality is punishable by up to three years in prison under "public moral laws." Humans fucking lions apparently still condoned.

LIBERIA

True to its American roots, Liberia also discriminates against gays. But unlike most African nations, sodomy is only punishable by a fine, making it an attractive option for travelers willing to do "gay for pay."

INDIA

In 2009, the Delhi High Court ruled the nation's homosexuality ban unconstitutional, but made the age of consent for homosexuals two years older than that for straights. It sounds hypocritical, but it's worked wonders for reducing gay teen pregnancies.

AFGHANISTAN

Since the fall of the Taliban, homosexuality no longer punishable by death (probably). So if that was the only thing stopping you from voguing down the streets of Kandahar, go right ahead!

DEMOCRATIC PEOPLE'S REPUBLIC OF KOREA

Though all public displays of affection are banned, the North Korean government "recognizes that many individuals are born with homosexuality as a genetic trait and treats them with due respect." Unfortunately, "due respect" means "if Kim Jong doesn't like what you did with his hair, you'll be standing in front of a firing squad." That also goes for styling his body double.

Slash Fiction

Despite countless reruns of *The Wizard of Oz,* television is no friend of Dorothy. Gay characters are few and far between, and they're definitely not getting any action on the screen. This is the driving force behind slash fiction, a genre that reimagines well-known TV characters as homosexuals with raging libidos. Today, anyone with a computer and the willingness to read television instead of watch it can experience their favorite characters living in an alternate universe devoid of silly hang-ups about things like sexual orientation and plot.

TV SHOWS
SORT BY: POPULARITY / NAME / GENRE

NAME	NUMBER OF STORIES	NAME	NUMBER OF STORIES
21 Jump Street	(392)	Highway to Heaven	(10)
227	(19)	Joanie Loves Chachi	(13)
Absolutely Fabulous	(1,500)	Knight Rider	(312)
Alf	(13)	Magnum P.I.	(44)
Alice	(29)	Mama's Family	(102)
Cagney & Lacey	(36)	Mary Hartman, Mary Hartman	(23)
Charles in Charge	(6)	Matlock	(0)
Designing Women	(9)	Mr. Belvedere	(17)
Donnie and Marie	(3)	Murder She Wrote	(18)
Dynasty	(4)	Night Court	(0)
Facts of Life	(158)	Partners in Crime	(3,250)
Facts of Life vol. 2		Punky Brewster	(4)
[Mrs. Garrett's Parlour]	(269)	Scarecrow and Mrs. King	(1,209)
Golden Girls	(430)	Three's Company	(57)
Golden Palace	(201)	Who's the Boss?	(148)
Hart to Hart	(27)	WKRP in Cincinnati	(8)

TV SHOWS » ALF » WET WILLIE

"WET WILLIE"
Series: ALF
Pairing: Willie/ALF
Submitted by: HungAngel12

[. . .] ALF spotted Willie approaching the garage and his green heart skipped a beat. Willie had been his friend and protector ever since his spaceship had crashed in the Tanners' backyard. Sure, Willie lost his temper every once in a while, but for the most part, you couldn't ask for a better companion. Except maybe a delicious tabby cat with a side of Melmacian mayo.

The screen door squeaked open. Willie looked even more frazzled than usual.

"Hey, Willie!"

"What is it, ALF?" Willie braced himself for bad news. Coming from ALF, it always was.

"I found some old leather chaps in a box under the workbench. Are they valuable?"

"Yes, they have a great deal of sentimental value. Why?"

"Because I ate them."

"ALF!"

"How was I supposed to know?" ALF replied, instantly on the defensive. "Besides, if you didn't want anyone touching them, you should have put your name on them."

"They did have my name on them. They were hand-embroidered."

"So you're 'Big Bottom Bill,'" ALF surmised.

"That was a long time ago, ALF." Willie spotted the last remnants of his carefree, leather daddy days scattered about the workbench. "Oh, they're ruined!"

"I think they were ruined when you bought them," ALF said, recalling the chaps' shoddy workmanship.

"Why do I even bother?" Willie lamented, slumping down on the ratty couch. ALF could see he'd really done it this time.

"I'm sorry, Willie."

"Oh, you're always sorry."

"Not always," ALF deadpanned. "Come on, Willie. Let me make it up to you."

"How could you possibly make it up to me?"

ALF could think of a few ways, but he wasn't sure Willie would like any of them, especially since most involved slow-roasting Lucky with shallots and a succulent port wine sauce. He had to stop thinking with his eight stomachs and do something Willie would truly appreciate. Suddenly, it dawned on him. "Hey, Willie!"

"What is it now, ALF?"

"Have you ever had a Melmacian Tickler?"

"No, ALF. I've never had a Melmacian Tickler. How in the world would I have had a Melmacian Tickler?"

"I don't know. Maybe you'd been to the rest stop just outside Neptune?"

Willie had had just about enough of ALF's foolishness. His face was flushed and his eyes burned with annoyed passion. "Willie, please," ALF pleaded, placing a fuzzy hand on Willie's knee. "Trust me."

"Oh, all right, ALF," Willie sighed. "I supposed there's nothing left for you to ruin."

ALF untucked Willie's shirt from his belt, revealing a taut set of abs. All that pent-up anxiety had given Mr. Tanner great muscle tone. Willie felt ALF's strong, three-fingered hands unfastening his belt.

"ALF, are you sure you know what you're doing?"

For once, ALF didn't have a wisecrack at the ready. He was totally focused on the task at hand. ALF yanked down Willie's boxer shorts, revealing his benefactor's rigid human cock. It made his mouth water more than reading "Garfield." ALF greeted his benefactor's penis with uncharacteristic savoir faire.

"Hey, Willie."

TV SHOWS » GOLDEN GIRLS » HOT FLASHES

"HOT FLASHES"
Series: The Golden Girls
Pairing: Dorothy/Rose/Blanche/Sophia
Submitted by: SilverYoni

[. . .] Blanche sashayed into the living room, eager to model her sequined bathing suit for the girls. "Well, what do you think of my new bikini?"

As always, Sophia didn't mince words. "What do I think? I've seen smaller disasters at the Bikini Atoll. At least there they handed out tinted goggles."

Blanche shrugged it off. She had learned long ago not to let the sassy Sicilian get to her. "You laugh, Sophia, but I'm going to look stunning in Dr. Fowler's Jacuzzi."

Dorothy felt a twinge of jealousy. Blanche was going on so many dates, Dorothy hardly got to see her anymore. "You and Dr. Fowler have been spending a lot of time with each other lately. Is it getting serious?"

"At her age?" Sophia blurted. "Take it from someone who knows: it's hard to be serious when you laugh every time you see each other naked."

"Well, let me put it this way," Blanche said, turning her shimmering backside to Sophia. "Let's just say these days I'm getting my checkups for free."

"You always get your checkups for free," Sophia retorted. "The only difference is these days it's by a doctor." Sensing she was getting some attention for a change, Sophia tried to impart some of her hard-earned wisdom. "You know, this reminds me of a story. Picture it: Sicily 1913. A young girl in her 'experimental phase' meets a buxom Swedish nurse named Ilsa—"

"Ma, please!" Dorothy knew she had to cut her mother off or they'd be hearing about her sexual exploits all night, including her imagined pre-WWII dalliance with Mrs. Mussolini. Blanche, however, wasn't even listening as she struggled to unfasten her bikini.

"Oh poop, this clasp is stuck. Dorothy, will you help?"

"Please! Go in the bedroom!" Sophia protested. "If I see your shriveled bosoms one more time, it will put me off prunes for good. And I need them to stay regular!"

"Don't pay any attention to her, Blanche. I'll fix it." Dorothy led the way to the bedroom. This was her chance to tell Blanche how she really felt. Sure, she wasn't rich like Dr. Fowler or young like that jai alai player who kept leaving his cesta basket in Blanche's backseat, but Dorothy could give her something no man could. Besides, she was a handsome woman, and Blanche was a slut. What was there to lose?

Blanche closed the bedroom door behind her and continued tugging at her suit. "Thank you so much, Dorothy. I think I see a sequin jammed in the clasp."

"What a surprise. You see something shiny and you want to take your top off."

Blanche wasn't surprised to hear a slut joke at her expense, but something about the way Dorothy said it made her suspect her roommate was testing the waters. Dorothy undid the clasp on Blanche's top. For just a moment, her hands lingered against Blanche's bronze skin. It was the only sign Blanche needed. "It doesn't have to be shiny."

"Oh yeah?" Dorothy said, smoldering with desire.

"Yeah!"

"Oh yeah?"

"Yeah!"

"Oh yeah—"

Dorothy grabbed Blanche by the shoulders and kissed her roughly. Blanche was caught off guard. She was usually the one to make the first move. Blanche felt the strength in Dorothy's hands. She was stronger than most of the men she dated. It turned her on, and that in turn turned Dorothy on. Dorothy couldn't believe what was happening. She started to worry she was making a mistake but stopped herself. *You've wanted this so long*, she thought. *Just enjoy it.* It was at that moment that Rose barged into the room. Blanche pulled away, but not before Rose saw everything.

"I'm so sorry! I thought you were in here making paper snowflakes for the Winter Ball," Rose blurted, her cheeks turning the same color as her name.

"Rose! Why in God's name would you think we were making snowflakes?"

"Sophia told me you were in here scissoring."

"Rose, you idiot!" Dorothy snapped. "Close the door and get in here!"

TV SHOWS » KNIGHT RIDER » GOOD IN THE CLUTCH

"GOOD IN THE CLUTCH"
Series: Knight Rider
Pairing: Michael Knight/KITT
Submitted by: HornyOrca

Michael was driving KITT down the road. Or rather, KITT was driving while Michael held the steering wheel so he felt important. They had been on the road for nearly eight hours, headed to a small town in West Virginia to investigate a series of art heists. It had been a while since either of them had spoken. Suddenly, KITT's anharmonic voice synthesizer broke the silence.

"Michael?"

"Yeah, KITT?"

"You want to fuck?"

Michael was unbuckling his seat belt before KITT even finished the question. "You got it, pal."

CHAPTER 7

For Sexperts Only

The Kitchen Sink of Sex

It is at this point—this sentence, in fact—where this book gets really FREAKY. Can you handle it? Not everyone can.

Though originality and self-expression are valued in every human endeavor from poetry to chili cook-offs, when it comes to sex those qualities are discouraged, if not shunned. You think being gay is tough? Imagine sitting your parents down and telling them you can only find sexual happiness dressed up like a giant baby. Or the funny looks you'd get at the baby supply store when you ask for a size XXXXL bonnet. You'll find most people simply aren't ready to embrace sexual exploration, much less try it themselves. Why is this?

The answer is that when it comes to sex, society tends to stick with the status quo. Which is Latin for "stop trying to take pictures of my feet, you creep."

Of course, society has every right to discourage sexual practices that are harmful or that deprive real giant-headed babies of bonnets. But when it comes to the stigma associated with broadening one's sexual horizons, the prevailing "if-it-ain't-broke-don't-fuck-it" attitude does a great disservice to our spirit of innovation—the very spirit that makes our species great. What if our primate ancestors had never tried the missionary position? Or if the Dutch had never invented foreplay? Where would today's "normal sex-havers" be then? If the guy in the man-sized diaper is any indication, probably having an awkward conversation with their parents.

Thankfully, there are a brave few willing to face ridicule or even Jerry Springer's studio audience in pursuit of their dreams. These are the heroic orgasmonauts exploring the farthest reaches of the known Pleasureverse, and they deserve our respect. Because without these sexual pioneers our species might be cumming, but we wouldn't be going anywhere.

Check "Other"

Ready to play the field? Not so fast. Before you do, you should know that Orgasm Meadow has a few black sheep.

Bisexuals

Bisexuals are the sexiest people on Earth because they know if you really love sex, you don't let a minor detail like gender prevent you from having it.

The bisexual pride flag, which some days prefers to be a pennant.

Only 2 to 3 percent of the population is sexually ambidextrous, making bisexuals the four-leaf clovers of the sex world. Meaning if you find one, consider yourself lucky! In fact, you should ask the bisexual if he or she wouldn't mind getting pressed between the pages of this book to give to your grandchildren someday. The bisexual will be flattered, and your grandkids will love it.

The only surefire way to spot a bisexual is to catch one speaking his or her secret language. Among their own kind, bisexuals talk in palindromes—words and phrases that fittingly go "both ways." We overheard this conversation at Radar, a popular bisexual club in Capac, Michigan.

> **MAN AT BAR**: *Yo, Banana Boy!*
>
> **BARTENDER**: *Huh?*
>
> **MAN AT BAR**: *Sex at noon taxes.*
>
> **BARTENDER**: *Ned, I am maiden.*
>
> **MAN AT BAR**: *Wow!*
>
> **BARTENDER**: *Party boobytrap.*
>
> **MAN AT BAR**: *No, still it's on. 'Ed is on no side.*

Did you understand that? If you did, you're totally bi.

Transgender Folk

Imagine being trapped in a mine. Your oxygen is running out and the only way you can survive is to smash through a rock wall. Now imagine the mine is your own body, the rock wall is traditional gender roles, and the oxygen is your hopes of a satisfying sex life. This is what it is like to be one of the untold millions of transgender Americans.

Ironically, the best way to spot a Tranny Smith Apple is by checking out its Adam's apple.

"Transgender" is an umbrella term for anyone who feels that they are something other than their biological sex. Medical professionals call this condition **Gender Identity Disorder (GID)**, and trying to classify all the different categories can be a hot mess.

Connect the following transgender categories to the appropriate face without offending anyone:

DRAG QUEEN	ANDROGYNE
DRAG KING	GIRLFAG
DRAG JACK	GUYDYKE

CROSS-DRESSER

The term "hermaphrodite" comes from Hermaphroditus, Greek god of hogging the remote and taking too long in the bathroom.

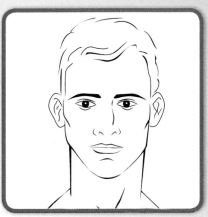

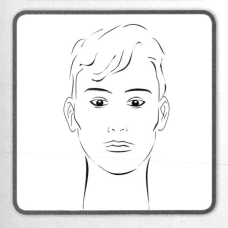

Intersex People

The term "intersex" is used to describe individuals born with genitalia that have both male and female characteristics. (People with this condition are sometimes referred to as hermaphrodites, but this label has been deemed offensive by the intersex community and fallen out of favor.) While having unique genitalia may sound like fun, intersex people are often made to feel ashamed of their bodies, something no one did better than little-known stand-up comedian Riff Rappaport.

RIFF RAPPAPORT

From 1989 until his murder at the hands of an angry mob of intersex individuals in 1994, Riff's inventive mix of humor, misconceptions, and flat-out lies about genital deformities raised awareness of intersexuality, though not always in a good way. Here is a partial transcript of Riff's hilariously tragic last set:

If you've ever yelled at yourself for leaving the toilet seat up · · · you might be a hermaphrodite.

If you refuse to pull over and ask for directions on your way to the SEX AND THE CITY movie · · · you might be a hermaphrodite.

If you eat bonbons out of a bowl shaped like a football helmet · · · you might be a hermaphrodite.

If you try to tell me my jokes are insensitive because hermaphrodites feel alienated enough without someone making fun of them · · · you might be a hermaphrodite.

If you keep telling me you prefer to be called "intersex" because "hermaphrodite" implies you have the same genitals as a tapeworm · · · you might be a hermaphrodite.

If you're angrily getting up from your chair and approaching the stage right now · · · you might be a hermaphrodite.

If you've got the balls to pick a fight at a comedy club, but one or both of them never descended · · · you might be a—oof! Hey, that hur—

(End of recording)

Eunuchs

Oh, hey there. I'm the eunuch section. Did you think the gay chapter was the only part of this book that was self-aware? It's not. I just have a little less to be aware of, on account of the fact I've been "edited." On the bright side (for you at least), I'm probably the only eunuch you'll ever bring home, given that chopping people's nuts off has been outlawed in most of the world. But there was a time when eunuchs were valued as harem guards, royal advisors, and castratos in Catholic Church choirs (though given the

It's sad to think we live in a world where trucks have nuts and some men don't.

heartbreak of involuntary castration, you'd think most eunuchs would be country singers). What was I saying? Oh right, my missing testicles. Sort of a hard thing to forget. My point is, these ˙ ʰings are e˙ ˙ɡher for eunuchs, now that we don't have all those c ˙tuniˈ ɔ think of it, do *you* have any eunuch jobs that nee ˙ giˈ ɔucks, I'll let you throw a football at my groin. No, ˌtill ˈ ˌ willing to "play ball," as it were. Basically, I'm just lˌ ˌr a résun˙ ˌ. Hey, where are you going? Is it something I said? You can't not hire me just because I'm a eunuch—that's discrimination. That's it, I'm suing you. No wait, I was just kidding. Come back!

FUCKTOID

Did you know Abraham Lincoln was avenged by a eunuch?

Thomas "Boston" Corbett was a sergeant in the Union Army who had castrated himself with a pair of scissors to avoid the sinful temptation of prostitutes. Following Lincoln's assassination in 1865, Corbett was sent to track down the fugitive John Wilkes Booth. Despite orders to take Booth alive, Corbett shot the deranged actor in the neck because, as he put it, "Providence directed me."

The moral of the story? You don't need nuts to be nuts.

Like his portrait, Boston Corbett was cropped below the waist.

Orgies

The credit for inventing the ultimate party game goes to the ancient Greeks, who conceived orgies as secret religious rites to honor Dionysus, the god of fertility and wine. Through dancing, drinking, and raucous group sex, worshipers of Dionysus sought to achieve a state of ecstasy in which they were temporarily freed from their earthly bodies. It worked—so well, in fact, that revelers often emerged from their euphoria to find they had torn apart wild animals with their bare hands and eaten the raw flesh. (Let this be a lesson—should you choose to host an orgy, be sure to have snacks!)

Like Jenga, but with naked people

In addition to being the spokes deity for fun things like sex and drunkenness, Dionysus was also the god of theater. So it isn't surprising to learn that Dionysus has been a scathing critic of the orgy scene, as evidenced by his weekly column in the *Mount Olympus Times-Picayune*:

IF YOU TRAVEL TO INDIA you may encounter hijras, gangs of transgendered buskers who make money by harassing people with dirty songs and dancing (like roving packs of RuPauls, without a pesky agent taking 10 percent). Hijras show up uninvited at weddings, births, and shop openings to capitalize on the superstition that hijras curse those who fail to appease them, but bring luck and good fortune to those who do.

WHAT TO DO: If hijras try to ruin your big day, don't let them! Their whole scam is based on the assumption they can embarrass you into forking over cash. So you have to show that you won't be humiliated. If it's your wedding day, pull down your pants and jiggle your junk in front of your new in-laws. If it's the grand opening of your frozen yogurt counter, start working the cash register with your penis. You may scare off a few customers, but those cross-dressing grifters will be "sari" they ever messed with you!

I'm "Dion" Over Here!

by Dionysus

Grand Duke Vytenis's Ascension Orgy

Castle of Novgorodok
c. A.D. 1295
Rating: 🍺🍺🍺🍺🍺

[. . .] Despite a rocky first act, the coronation festivities built to a tantalizing climax as the Grand Duke ordered his three wives to strip and submit themselves to a trio of hill goats. The lead goat, ably played by Land Master Bruno's prize short-hair Jasper, did not disappoint, thrusting and heaving his woolly haunches like the great Pan himself. With the moans of the Vytenis women and the clanging of Jasper's bell building to an orgasmic crescendo, it seemed as though this was going to be a gangbang for the ages. And then . . . nothing. In some of the worst orgy blocking this reviewer has ever had the misfortune of witnessing, the satisfied goats simply meandered off stage, pausing only briefly to chew the scenery. Herein lay the fatal flaw of the Grand Duke's latest effort. What's the point of putting goats in an orgy if you don't tear them apart and eat them?

Pope Alexander VI Presents: The Ballet of Chestnuts

Palace of the Vatican
October 30, 1501
Rating: 🍺🍺🍺

[. . .] Following a procession before the pontiff that lagged like a drunken caterpillar, fifty courtesans danced with the banquet guests, the wenches brightly garbed at first and then not at all. But other than Pope Alexander's bold choice of venue (and the complementary ruby-encrusted fanny paddle), the whole affair sagged. Sensing his cue, the pope's bastard son Don Cesare began scattering roasted chestnuts about the palace floor. Lowering a candelabrum to illuminate the errant nuts, he then ordered the whores to pick them up . . . with their mouths. They did so greedily, giving the pope and his retinue ample opportunity to admire their noble parts, a spectacle this reviewer won't soon forget.

But roasted chestnuts? How about eating some nonroasted wild animals? Doesn't anyone throw *orgies* anymore?

Formula One Chief Max Mosley's Nazi Concentration Camp Bondage Orgy

Max Moseley's Chelsea Torture Flat
March 28, 2008
Rating: Too soon.

Ray and Margaret's Backyard Bacchanalia

Memorial Day, 2009
Rating: 🍺

[. . .] Despite a promising run time of "Noon–???" and a "decadent" amount of mayonnaise in the potato salad, this so-called bacchanalia failed to live up to its ambitious billing. Though courteous and charming hosts in their own right, Margaret and Ray simply haven't the talent nor the wanton depravity needed to host a bachelorette party, much less a full-blown orgy. Also, with regard to the ambrosia salad, this deity doesn't remember the food of the gods having quite so many marshmallows. (But that didn't stop me from going back for seconds!)

Wildo's Retreat

In the seventies and early eighties, there were more functioning sex clubs in New York City than there were Ray's Famous Pizzas. But without a doubt the greatest club of all was Wildo's Retreat, located in the heart of the Swingers' District. Featuring a nude waitstaff, all-you-can-eat edible underwear, and twice-daily hosings-down, Wildo's Retreat was *the* place for public displays of friction. And every night, Wildo would take a stroll right through the middle of it, basking in his life's work. Can you spot him?

L.L.Beast

A Catalog for Animal Lovers

A.

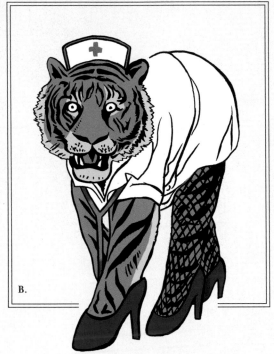

B.

A. GOAT COP, BAD COP Whether it's Sergeant Billy or Officer Nanny, you'd better spread 'em when they trot up in this sexy uniform. You broke the laws of nature, so shut up and listen when they bleat out your rights.

KEY FEATURES
- Edible cotton/nylon blend
- Comes in navy or black (only one of you is color blind!)
- One size fits around all four-chambered stomachs

ITEM #TA259553 $49.85

B. TIG*E.R.* You better be brave, because this tiger is a very naughty nurse! Nurse Tiger will take your pulse right before she slashes your heart out. An apple a day most definitely won't keep Nurse Tiger away from giving you a bloody sponge bath. *Catalog and Web only.*

KEY FEATURES
- Stethoscope, even though your pounding heart will be audible without it
- Sensible shoes
- Anal thermometer . . . so hold still!

ITEM #TA233493 $61.19

C.

D.

C. I GOT YOU, BABE Finally, nipple clamps that everyone in the animal kingdom can enjoy. Your pig can embrace its gluttony by clamping down all its teats at once! No more rotating around the traditional two clamps—your pig will appreciate a simultaneous nipple tweak for all twelve teats. And it will go hog wild for the fashionable leather collar.

KEY FEATURES
- Stainless-steel clamps and chains, easy to wash mud off
- Removable clamps in case your pig has fewer than twelve teats. You can use the extras on yourself!
- Clover clamps coming soon, pending PETA approval

ITEM #TQ776912 $80.32
(that's only $6.69 per clamp!)

Also available in Dungeoness Crab
ITEM #TQ774562 $36.78

D. JUNGLE FEVER Put your aggressive hippo into submission with the ultimate toy made just for her. This one-of-a-kind gag ball is four feet in diameter and made of 100 percent American steel. Fitting just behind the teeth, hippo will be drooling a river all its own. Keep your hungry hungry hippo begging for more!

KEY FEATURES
- Adjustable strap
- Waterproof
- Grass flavored

ITEM #TG679148 $749.66

URBAN LEGENDS of SEX

We've all heard them. Whispered tales of sexual experimentation gone horribly awry, usually with devastating consequences. One is tempted to dismiss them as freak accidents or tall tales. But the fact that they all happened to "a friend of a friend" makes you wonder if this sort of crazy shit is true. The answer may scare you into never being sexy again.

DIRTY DOG

THE LEGEND: Curious about sex, a lonely teenage girl stuck a frozen hot dog up her vagina. When she tried to get it out, she couldn't! The hot dog had gone too far inside her, and she had to go to the hospital to have it removed.

True or false: **TRUE!**

WHAT REALLY HAPPENED: This legend is based on a terrifying chain of events that happened to Jenny Fillmore of Boulder, Colorado. What started as a midnight snack turned into an all-you-can eat humiliation buffet, served up with a pair of warm tongs.

Jenny, a shy freshman at John Elway High School, had been craving a hot dog all day. When she pulled one out of the freezer she couldn't help but notice it was the same size and shape as the penis illustrated in her health book. Her curiosity piqued, Jenny smuggled the uncooked wiener to her bedroom. She'd planned to let it thaw out to what she guessed was penis temperature, but when her dad knocked on the door, Jenny panicked. Not knowing how to explain having a frozen hot dog in her room, she stuffed it up her vagina. When the coast was clear Jenny tried to retrieve it, but there was nothing to grab on to. The frankfurter had gone frankly-further than she'd wanted it to. Jenny screamed in horror as she realized she'd become the human bun to this hot dog from hell.

When Jenny arrived at the hospital she wasn't sure what to tell the ER staff. Luckily, removing frozen hot dogs from vaginas was one of the first things they taught in med school. Expert hands reversed

Jenny's plight, but the school bully Kenneth "Swirly" Giles happened to be at the same hospital getting treated for a minor stomach explosion caused by mixing Pop Rocks and Coke. He heard why Jenny was there and told all of his friends shortly before he died from cherry blood bubbles.

PEANUT BUTTER SURPRISE

THE LEGEND: This guy totally walked in on another guy putting peanut butter on his dick and letting his dog lick it off.

True or false: **TRUE!**

WHAT REALLY HAPPENED: The peanut butter pervert was Jonathan Duke of Downers Grove, Illinois. But it wasn't peanut butter, it was Nutella, The Original Hazelnut Spread.

Jonathan had been having a bad day. No one had remembered it was his birthday, not even the cute receptionist Julia. Frustrated by loneliness and an extended romantic dry spell, Jonathan decided to turn to some creature comfort after work. He knew his Boston terrier, Sandy, loved the rich and creamy taste of Nutella. So much, in fact, that she would hardly notice whether she was licking it off his finger or his lonely birthday penis. Convinced his beloved pooch wouldn't be traumatized, Jonathan slathered his member with Nutella's chocolaty goodness. Soon the dark kitchen was filled with the sounds of Sandy's lapping and Jonathan's ecstatic moans.

Little did Jonathan know his friends, coworkers, parents, grandparents, and even the cute receptionist Julia were hiding in the den, waiting to throw him a surprise birthday party. After hearing strange sounds coming from the kitchen, the well-wishers decided to investigate. Clicking on the lights, they shouted something along the lines of "Surpriii—oh my GOD!" and Jonathan saw both his dignity and his erection disappear before his eyes. Even the dog was mortified, but only because she'd missed the last heavenly dollop of Nutella on Jonathan's hazelnut nutsack.

RODENT TO PERDITION

THE LEGEND: A certain famous actor had a live gerbil up his anus.

True or false: **TRUE!**

WHAT REALLY HAPPENED: The actor was Clarence T. Conway of the Stony Brook Players and the gerbil belonged to his son Rudy's first-grade class. Rudy had volunteered to take care of Yu-Gi-Oh: The Gerbil (whose name had been decided by a class vote) over the Christmas break.

One night, Clarence tossed and turned as he tried to rest up for the next day's performance of *Wicked* at a local retirement home. Remembering an old actor's trick for beating insomnia, he drank a whole bottle of gin. One thing led to another, and before long Clarence had inserted Yu-Gi-Oh up his classically trained keester. In addition to being uncomfortable, the shock of having a live creature inside him sobered Clarence up instantly. Unfortunately, little Yu-Gi-Oh wasn't going anywhere. Finally, the tired thespian coaxed the gerbil out of himself with an empty toilet paper roll and a few pieces of popcorn.

The next day, Clarence was in the middle of a heartfelt rendition of "A Sentimental Man" when he felt something other than sentiments stirring deep inside him. Committed to his craft, Clarence soldiered on with the performance. But just as the song was building to its emotional climax, five hairless pink gerbil babies scurried down the Wizard of Oz's pant leg and scattered about the dayroom. Yu-Gi-Oh had birthed them in Clarence's rectum, and his unsuspecting warmth had made them strong and healthy (except for the sixth gerbil, which died and remained inside Clarence). Several seniors called the performance "nice."

A Brief Conversation with a Dominatrix

(and her slave)

YEAH LET'S TALK ABOUT BDSM. WHAT DOES BDSM STAND FOR, SLAVE? Bondage and Discipline/Sadomasochism. VERY GOOD. GET UNDER THE QUEENING STOOL. BDSM HAS GOTTEN A LOT OF NEGATIVE PUBLICITY OVER THE YEARS, AND THAT'S BULLSHIT. WHEN BDSM IS DONE RIGHT IT'S ABOUT TRUST IT'S A BOND THAT GOES BEYOND WHAT A REGULAR RELATIONSHIP CAN OFFER. IT'S ABOUT CARING AND UNDERSTANDING AND TRUSTING LIMITS. In a safe, sane, consensual manner. SHUT UP, SLAVE! DID I TELL YOU YOU COULD TALK? DID I TELL YOU YOU COULD OPEN THAT FOUL LITTLE TRAP OF YOURS? ANSWER ME! No, Mistress. GO GET YOUR COLLAR YOU DON'T DESERVE TO BE UNDER MY ANUS RIGHT NOW YOU ARE SO OUT OF LINE. ANYWAYS, IT IS A PARTNERSHIP WHERE BOTH SIDES HAVE TO EARN THE OTHER'S RESPECT IT'S HARD WORK. Arf. Arf. GOOD PUPPY. HE WASN'T ALWAYS MY SLAVE. HE STARTED AS A SUB, BUT AFTER SEVERAL YEARS, WE REALIZED THAT WE COULD TAKE IT TO THE NEXT LEVEL. DOWN, GET DOWN! WHO TOLD YOU YOU COULD JUMP UP? WAS IT ME? NO! YOU NEED TO BE PUNISHED! Arf! GET ME MY WHIP. *(Dog whine.)* ANYWAYS, I FEEL SATISFIED MAKING MY SLAVE HAPPY, AND THERE ARE VERY SPECIFIC WAYS TO DO IT. THAT'S A GOOD BOY. NOW HOLD STILL! *(Whips.)* Arf! SHUT UP! I'M GOING TO GIVE YOU THREE MORE LASHES, AND IF I HEAR A PEEP FROM YOU I WILL LOCK YOU IN THE PANTRY! *(Three more whips.)* IT'S GOING THE EXTRA MILE TO DISCOVER ANOTHER PERSON'S NEEDS. I'VE TRIED VANILLA SEX, AND IT WASN'T INTIMATE ENOUGH FOR ME WAS IT, SLAVE? Grrrrr. THAT'S RIGHT. GET BACK UNDER THE QUEENING STOOL.

Fetishes!

Still haven't found that sexy someone? It might be that someone is a something. Fetishes are sexual fixations involving any object, situation, or body part not typically considered "sexy." As it turns out, just about anything can get your rocks off. Now get out there and get turned on!

1. Dendrophilia: Trees
2. Acrotomophilia: Amputations
3. Agalmatophilia: Statues
4. Urolagnia: Urinating and/or being urinated on
5. Aquaphilia: Water
6. Gerontophilia: Elderly people
7. Trichophilia: Hair
8. Lactaphilia: Breast milk
9. Autonepiophilia: Being a baby
10. Somnophilia: Sleeping or unconscious people
11. Mucophilia: Mucus
12. Chremastistophilia: Being robbed or held up
13. Coulrophilia: Clowns
14. Coprophilia: Feces
15. Formicophilia: Being crawled on by insects
16. Phalloorchoalgolagnia: Being hit in the balls
17. Mysophilia: Decaying things
18. Algolagnia (aka masochism): Pain
19. Necrophilia: Cadavers
20. Dacryphilia: Crying
21. Pyrophilia: Fire
22. Retifism: Shoes
23. Objectum sexuality: Inanimate objects
24. Plushophilia: Stuffed toys or people in animal costumes
25. Libriredimiophilia: Book bindings

The Love Ness

I've devoted my life to her. Or him. The gender has never been confirmed. But I'll call it a her because of the curves. The mouthwatering curves. Sometimes I'll trace her body in the air with my hand. I follow the long slender neck down into wetness, back up across a sweet hump and then back into wetness, and then along a second hump just under the water. When my hand gets to that submerged hump I have to think about something else; otherwise I'll get an instant hard-on.

My last girlfriend, Rita, is actually the one who told me about her. She had just returned from a business trip to Scotland. I zeroed in on her succulent, pouty lips as they formed the words. "Loch"—it was as if her mouth was readying itself for a blow job—"Ness"—and then snapped back into a satisfied smile—" . . . Monster. We didn't see it. Joel. Joel? Are you listening?"

Of course I was, Rita. You'd just introduced me to the love of my life.

I developed tunnel vision for this sea creature. I learned everything I could about my sweet Scottish monster. I was no longer interested in Rita. Especially after she declined to get a tattoo of Nessie on her upper thigh.

I've stopped being able to orgasm without thinking of her. When her gorgeous horned head breaks the surface of the water I lose control. I don't like to use the word "fetish." I don't like the sound of it. It sounds like a soggy vegetable. I worry that's what my fascination with Nessie has become: limp broccoli rabe.

My only hope is that Nessie is real. Why else would she be haunting me like this? She's a siren singing me to shipwreck . . . or paradise. I bought a ticket to Scotland today. One-way.

*   *   *

Virgin Atlantic coach sucks ass. Don't fly Virgin across the ocean unless you're Dick Branson. It's a rich man's airline with a miserable coach section to fly the help. I'm average height, but my knees were still crunched against the seat in front of me. For the first time in my life I felt claustrophobic. I waited for the stewards to come by every couple hours and pop ice creams and snacks into our mouths like baby chicks. Then I forced sleep on my cramped muscles. I imagined the smallness of the seat was just the pressure of the water as I sank farther and farther below to meet my love.

In my dream everything is pitch-black except for an iridescent glow in the distance. It pulses and I am pulled in like a planet. I don't worry about breathing because the energy from the light is my new life source. I'm also dressed in a black vintage three-piece suit with a dusty orange tie and a gold pocket watch. Not important, but I look good. The water is freezing until I get closer to the light where I feel a sensual warmth. At first I think I peed myself, because I always have to pee in my dreams. But the embarrassment goes away as a rush of even warmer water passes over me. I'm in her aura, lit up in a soft neon green, and in front of me floats Nessie.

She's radiant. Saying she resembles a plesiosaur is not accurate. She is her own species. She is shaped like a serpent on the ends and a camel in the middle. Her body is covered in iridescent scales that shimmer like peacock feathers. Her flippers are large diamond discs with fringe like a prehistoric buckskin jacket. Her neck is long, almost six feet, and slender. She curves it in the water with the elegance of a ribbon twirler, quick Os and Ss, sideways 8s, she could be spelling something out for me, but I am distracted by her eyes. They are as large as a cow's and neon green, the source of all the light. In a flash her neck wraps around me and guides me to her. She pins me against her torso with her diamond fin. Her flank is quivering. It feels like a school of fish is still alive inside her, swimming rhythmically. It's electrifying. I've never felt this excited in my life. I'm shaking uncontrollably. My skin is covered in goose bumps and my pants are bursting. She is face to face with me. I'm inches away from glowing eyes and a delicate snout and mouth accented by two small horns.

I smile. And she smiles. It's a smile that I know. It's sort of a cross between my first dog Buster's grin and Rita's. Then she rubs her cheek against mine and it's soft. Her scales are made out of some sort of water-resistant velvet. I love her. I feel amazing. Sexually charged, confident, and peaceful. I don't want to be anywhere else but here, underwater with Nessie. She knows it too. She runs her long neck down my body and licks at my crotch.

"Flight attendants, prepare the cabin for landing." Thank God.

*   *   *

I picked the cheapest and most crowded tour bus to Loch Ness. I didn't want to make friends. I didn't want anyone to notice that when the bus left, I wasn't on it. I kept my head down and listened to the tour guide.

"Now if you look out your window there to your right, you'll see an outhouse. That's where J.K. Rowling lived when she was first writing the Harry Potter book. We'll pull over so you can all touch it."

It was difficult to contain myself as the bus inched slowly toward my love's lair. I could almost smell her. It was a freshwater lake, but Nessie was salty, and I could detect the faintest scent of brine in the air. Brine and sweat

The brochure of the tour had a cartoon Nessie. Green and cheerful, winking. Scaling her great mythology down to a commercial. They have no idea. No one knows Nessie as I do. None of those scientists with all their sonar scans, hydrophones, and motorboats have a clue who Nessie is. I am the expert. I know that she is real. I am constantly in touch with her. On a subconscious level. A spiritual level. If I ever meet one of her hunters, I will personally punch him in the face. Because Nessie hates the sonar scans. She has incredibly sensitive ears.

Her home was even more beautiful in person. The lake was a steel sword cutting through miles of green hills. The tourists snapped a few pictures and tumbled back on the bus to go to a pub where J.K. Rowling got drunk for the first time. I was already drunk, on salty Nessie air. I ducked behind a tree until the sound of the bus engine faded into the distance. The lake was still. Everything was. Nessie, I thought, don't make me wait. We're alone now.

But that's exactly what she did. Three hours went by. I thought I saw something in the water, but it was just a bird skimming the surface. Five hours went by. I fell asleep staring into the darkness looking for her green glow. I dreamt I was back in my vintage suit. Only this time there was no light in the black water. No life source from which to breathe. I felt a warmth again and I thought maybe it was her. But now it was my own piss. I hadn't moved from my spot since the bus left. I was afraid I might miss her. At dawn the sun lit up the gray sky to a dull silver. I sat up and stared back at the lake. It was serene. My chest hurt. I told myself it was because I was alone in a foreign country with pissed jeans and an empty stomach. But I knew the real reason was heartbreak.

I stood up and began to walk back up toward the road. I wasn't sure what I was going to do next. Find some food. Maybe hike around the lake a bit and try to find her from the other side. Perhaps make my way back home. Call Rita.

And that's when I heard her. Something in the water was moving. I heard a cry. It sounded like Chewbacca. I hate to compare her to that, but that's exactly what it sounded like. It was guttural and high-pitched at the same time.

I turned around and there she was in the lake. But she looked different. Her luxurious peacock-colored velvet scales were replaced by a leathery olive green skin that wrinkled across her body like a sick elephant's. Her neck was much shorter, only about three feet. And her head was smaller and less shapely, like a nub without the horns. Those magic green eyes that I loved were replaced by two beady black ones. I tried to make out an expression on her face, one of love, or at least recognition. But it was empty.

I was torn. I was disappointed that this monster didn't match up to the love of my dreams. But I was also overjoyed that she was real. Validating my sanity. She wailed out to me again and pounded her tiny head in the water, creating ripples that crawled right up to my shoe. I knew that she wanted me to come to her. I hesitated. If only that J.K. Rowling pub were closer so I could work up some serious beer goggles. On the hotness scale of one to ten for mythical beasts, this one was rocking a four. I'm not a snob, but when you're used to fantasizing to a ten you sort of have to retrain your brain.

I locked eyes with her. She held my gaze with a blank stare. It was now or never. I dove face-first into the water and swam frantically. I'm not a spectacular swimmer, but I have finessed the doggy paddle.

The water was cold and it numbed me to my core. I opened my eyes, surprised by how clear it was. I could see Nessie gently paddling her unusually tiny fins. Her body was lumpy and awkward. I swam up next to her, unsure what to do. So I treaded. She lowered her small head close to my face. She didn't smell like salt at all. She smelled like rotten fish. I shuddered back a wave of nausea. And that's when I saw it. The smile. Just like my fantasy. A little Buster, a little Rita, but all Nessie.

I reached out and held on to her leathery neck so I wouldn't drown.

She howled again, but this time it was softer. I swung my leg over her back and straddled one of her humps. I could feel something moving inside Nessie, but it wasn't fish. There was an eruption in the water directly behind me. The sulfur smell almost knocked me unconscious as I became the first human to witness the Loch Ness monster farting. I smiled. Nessie began to swim farther out. Her muscles moved under me. I squeezed my legs tighter around Nessie's back, my crotch getting massaged from the movement of the hump. Instinctively the creature sensed she was carrying an extra bulge. She snapped her head around and buried her snout in my crotch. I gasped. She flicked her head up and licked me with a catlike tongue and then gunned it to the nearest shore.

She dropped me on a tiny patch of beach closed in by thick trees. She laboriously waddled her bulky body next to mine and wasted no time.

I threw off my soiled jeans and boxers and offered up my nervous cock. I was shaking with excitement and fear.

Nessie wrapped her tiny mouth all the way down to the base of my cock and held tight. She then swirled her sandy tongue around my shaft like a machine. I never could have dreamed it would feel this good. Soft, firm, rough, and relentless. Round and round, her tongue had a life of its own. Her eyes stared dead into mine. If her tongue wasn't so amazing I would have lost my erection. I closed my eyes and conjured up my fantasy Nessie. The colorful elegant beast lifted her gorgeous head above the water, and I came uncontrollably into the real one's mouth. I opened my eyes and watched Nessie suck out every last drop. She was starving for it. She pulled back and licked up and down my shaft in case she missed some.

"Ease up, Nessie!"

She let go of my cock and stared at me again with her black eyes. Only now there was a spark of green in them. She smiled. And I knew. Flying back to the United States was going to be even more cramped.

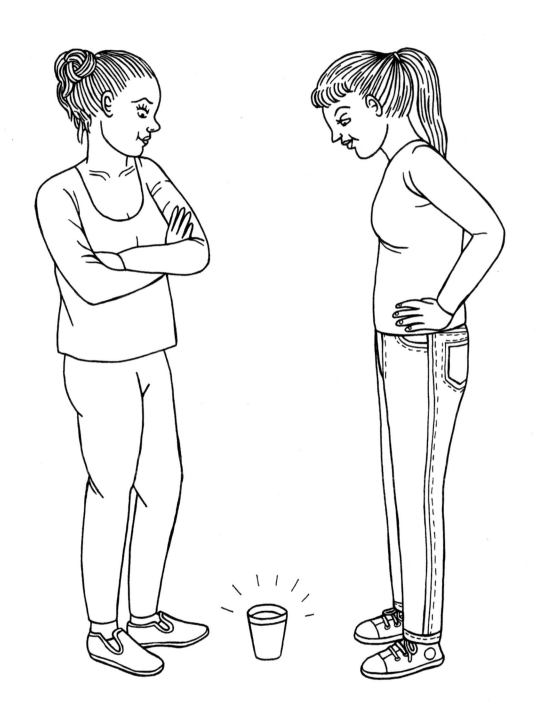

CHAPTER 8

The Dark Side of Sex

The Dark Side of Sex:
This Is Where the Tragic Happens

Life would be so much easier if sex were always a good thing, be it a physical bond between souls or a pleasant way to kill ten minutes until something good comes on TV. Unfortunately, sex sometimes kills far more than time. Sometimes it kills *people*.

Did a chill just run down your spine? Good. Because if there's one thing this chapter should teach you it's that SEX IS DANGEROUS. Done wrong, it can ruin your reputation, your career, your future, your glass-bottom boat, your cashmere sweater, and scariest of all, your own genitals.

Before switching over to whistles, many women carried a **rape theremin** *to scare off assailants.*

Did another chill just run down your spine? Even better. Because the first time you have sex, you start down a dangerous path. A few wrong turns and you could wind up at a grimy brothel in *Prostitutionville*, a secluded farmhouse in *Bestialitychusetts*, or a beautiful prewar townhouse with a backyard in *Pedophiladelphia* (real estate there tends to be a buyer's market).

Did you just get a third, even chillier chill? That might be overdoing it a little. You don't want to get too many butterflies in your penis or you'll fall victim to another sexual nightmare: impotence. Fail to perform in the sack, and word of your sexual mediocrity will spread like mildfire.

The point is, there's plenty to be scared of when it comes to sex. And in some ways, that only makes it hotter.

HIV/AIDS

One of the most devastating STDs is the fucking human immuno-deficiency virus, also known as fucking HIV. Spread by unprotected sex or needle sharing, this shit-stick of a virus attacks and destroys white blood cells, hampering one's ability to fight off infection and other, less cocksucking viruses. Then, like a real asshole, HIV progresses to its final shitty stage, known as Acquired Immune Deficiency Syndrome (AIDS). AIDS is characterized by dark skin blotches, dementia, difficulty breathing, and being even more of a god-awful bloodfart than HIV (if you can imagine such a thing).

Because AIDS (which, it should be noted, is a cunty shitstain) is both fatal and incurable, nothing has done more to discourage people from practicing "free love," which ended after the 1970s because

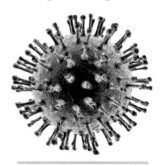

Fucking asshole.

of the party-killing evil dickbag AIDS. Thankfully, scientists are hard at work developing new drugs that will not only cure the pus-guzzling blight on humanity that is HIV, but kill it in the most slow and agonizing way possible (since that's what it fucking deserves, the scum-sucking sack of shit). In the meantime, research continues, and people everywhere hope that AIDS dies of AIDS.

HOW MANY PEOPLE HAVE YOU SLEPT WITH?

It's probably more than you think. Because when you sleep with someone, you sleep with everyone that person has slept with, and everyone those people have slept with, and so on and so forth. In fact, your list of partners is so long that if you lined them up single file and walked them over a cliff, the death march would never end, because the people at the back of the line would be having babies . . . with you. Because apparently, you're the type of sicko who gets turned on by forcing people to march off cliffs.

Sexually Transmitted Diseases (STDs)

If your genitals are burning, it's not because someone is talking about them. Chances are you've picked up one of nature's little hitchhikers, and now that it's riding shotgun in your reproductive system, it's decided maybe it'll go wherever you're going. DON'T LET IT! Unlike the people who transmit them, STDs never just wait until you fall asleep and sneak out of your apartment. You've got to kick them to the microscopic curb with the help of a bouncer named medicine. Remember: love is a battlefield, but sex is all-out biological warfare. Wear your protective gear, or pieces of you are going to start melting and falling off.

STD	NICKNAMES	WHAT IT LOOKS LIKE	WHAT IT FEELS LIKE	FAMOUS SUFFERER	OOZE FACTOR
GONORRHEA	The clap, the drip, Señor Leaky		Worse than having your ear cut off		●●●●●
SYPHILIS	The great imitator, the clown prince of STDs		Not that bad, really, until the part when you die		●
GENITAL HERPES (HSV)	Love blisters, passion tattoos, boyfriend barnacles		Avast! This scourge be a prickly albatross about ye genitals, matey		●●●

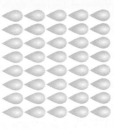

(Argentinian teardrops)

NONE
(But its brother Hep C totally knows Pamela Anderson)

Your mom

A magical dragon hoarding gold thumbtacks in your urethra

Not that bad, really, until the part when you die

A million tiny lobsters nibbling on your dignity

Someone playing the bongos on your liver

A creature growing inside you for nine months, at which point it bursts out of your vagina and starts eating all your money

The silent disease, the secret of the ooze, Princess Chlamydia of Drippington Manor

Lady lumps, the cauliflower patch, Farmer Pete

Crabs, poverty bugs, welfare weevils, pube surfers

Hepatitis not-A, C, D, or E, Hep Cat

Bun in the oven, kickworm

CHLAMYDIA

GENITAL WARTS (HPV)

GENITAL LICE

HEPATITIS B

FEMALE STOMACH PARASITE (FSP)

Sex as Work:
When Blow Jobs Become a Blo-cupation

Though getting paid to have sex may sound like a dream gig, anything you do because it's your job has a way of becoming a lot less fun. There are three main types of sex work, each with its own job description and perks. The dress code tends to be pretty lax.

Erotic "Dancing"

*A **real cake** that size would have cost more than the stripper.*

Though erotic dancers insist they're "artists," their performances are little more than group ogling set to music. Add some clothes to the choreography and you'll see just how many art lovers stick around for the next song. To be fair, **strip shows** do possess a certain avant-garde quality given that they can happen anywhere: a table, a pole, a giant cake, the ever-changing contours of the human lap. Not even Shakespeare could have imagined that much of the world being a stage.

Prostitution

*As a rule, **pimping** works out better for rides than it does for women.*

If you're willing to go the extra mile for a little more cash, then you may want to try your hand, mouth, penis, vagina, or any other body part you're willing to have violated at the sex-for-money racket. One of the few female-dominated industries, prostitution is the world's oldest profession, which isn't surprising considering every woman is born with a working storefront.

Like exotic "dancers," some prostitutes sugarcoat their job descriptions by saying they provide "massages" or "bodywork." This is absolutely correct. As far as customer satisfaction is concerned, prostitutes give some of the best, most relaxing massages known to man.

But be advised: in many parts of the world prostitution is illegal, and hookers turn to **pimps** for protection, fur care tips, and unsolicited physical motivation. (Think of them as "broken-life coaches.") In return, pimps receive a generous share of the profits, and if they're true 2 da pimpin' game, the remaining share of the profits. For this reason, prostitute retirement plans often rely on being a **hooker with a heart of gold**, meeting a wealthy businessman, and being whisked away to a life that doesn't involve buying penicillin in bulk. Unfortunately, this seldom happens, as any hooker with a real golden heart would see it confiscated by her pimp and melted down into teeth and goblets.

FUCKTOID

In cities like Amsterdam and Las Vegas, prostitutes have formed their own trade unions, a movement that ironically means dealing with even more scabs.

Pornography

You've jiggled your breasts for Japanese business-men, you've had more sailors inside you than a *Nimitz*-class aircraft carrier, but despite all your efforts, you still don't feel like you're getting enough attention. If this is you, then you have what it takes to be a star! No, not a real star. A **porn star**.

As celebrities of the sex industry, porn stars enjoy the skin-crawling satisfaction that comes with knowing thousands of people have stared at you while masturbating (and a few of them may have actually paid for it!). Yet for all the exposure, there are quite a few downsides to being a smutsperson: the constant anal bleaching, the lurking possibility of contracting an STD, and perhaps worst of all,

*Yet another **hot, delicious pizza** that will probably get eaten by the crew.*

never getting to eat any of the freshly delivered pizza that so often introduces "extra sausage" into the plot.

On the bright side, adult film performers get to pick a fun porn name. In recent years, most aspiring stars have done this using the Zmenckamynkcis formula. Developed in 1980 by porn producer and mathematician Bob Zmenckamynkcis, the formula provided a group of people not known for their career savvy with an easy recipe for concocting a memorable nom de splooge:

$$fp + ST = Pn$$

(name of first pet) + (street you grew up on) = (your porn name)

The dog and street that launched a thousand money shots.

For erotic performers the world over, Zmenckamynkcis's formula proved a veritable Ellis Island (somewhere Zmenckamynkcis's ancestors had obviously bypassed). Overnight, fresh young talent like Mittens Morningside, Nibbles Elm, Shadow Pudding, and even Ron Jeremy became household names, all thanks to Zmenckamynkcis's earth-shaking discovery.

Yet for all its triumphs, the Zmenckamynkcis formula is not perfect. Like Einstein's theory of relativity, the pet/street paradigm has been shown to break down under extreme conditions, at which point it can produce some of the least sexy porn names ever conceived. Names like:

- Rascal Martin Luther King Jr. Boulevard
- Rags West 34th
- Buster Service Ramp

It is for this reason that we picked up where Zmenckamynkcis left off. After five years of exhaustive research and field testing, we are happy to announce an even better method:

The Sexy Book of Sexy Sex's
IMPROVED PORN NAME FORMULA

[
FAVORITE ALCOHOLIC BEVERAGE
+
BIGGEST INSECURITY
=
YOUR IMPROVED PORN NAME
]

Examples:

- Chardonnay Mathematics
- Mudslide Commitment
- Gimlet Stutter
- Margarita Halitosis
- Julep Incontinence
- Fuzzy Navel Eczema
- Singlemalt Bald Head
- Curaçao Bigvagina

Hopefully, you'll never have to use this ground-breaking erotic discovery that will determine the names behind beaded curtains in video stores for the next thousand years. But should you decide to break into show-it-all business, at least the guy holding the boom mic will know what to call you when he tells you there isn't any pizza left.

MY IMPROVED PORN NAME IS:

_____

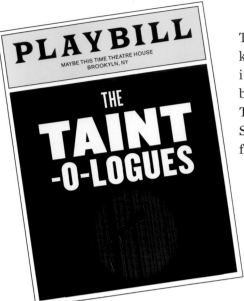

PLAYBILL

MAYBE THIS TIME THEATRE HOUSE
BROOKYLN, NY

THE TAINT -O-LOGUES

Though sex has inspired great art, it's also been known to inspire terrible art. One of the most infamous examples is *The Taint-o-logues*, directed by Liz Rosenthal. It premiered in 2002 at the Maybe This Time Theatre House on Ninth Street in Park Slope, Brooklyn. There are twenty-six monologues from that production. Here are the best three.

My Taint Is a Phoenix

My taint is tiny. It's special. It's mine.
You can steal my heart, but you're not taking my taint.
You can rip apart my dignity, but my taint will remain intact.
You can do me in the anus, but just you try to penetrate my taint!
I hold on to my taint fiercely, because you. can't. have. it.

(Audience whooping and applause.)

I'll never forget the first time I saw my taint. I was thirteen. I was in my bedroom with my mother's hand mirror. I was on my back, legs spread, gazing at my treasure. Nestled like an island between two black holes. It was a constant between unknowns. I touched my pinky finger to my taint and pretended it was a castaway on Taint Island. My pinky traced its small island quarters, and quickly developed rock fever. Pinky jumped frantically for help and caught Ring Finger's attention. He was on his way.

(Audience giggles.)

Together they made a home on Taint Island, exploring the parameters back and forth endlessly. But before they could get off the island, my mother walked in on me.

She was livid. Horrified. Annoyed. And most of all: jealous. She grabbed the mirror away from me and screamed, "I DON'T WANT TO EVER SEE YOU PLAYING WITH YOUR TAINT AGAIN!"

(Audience is hushed. Someone sniffles.)

And I didn't. For forty-two years. Four taint-free decades passed me by. My taint was nothing but a ghost down there. Floating silently between my anus and vagina. Haunting my prepubescent memories.

After my mother died I had to clean out her house. The first thing I found was that hand mirror. I missed my mom, but now I missed my taint even more. I closed the door to her bedroom and arranged myself on her bed. I was scared of what I might see. Would my taint still look the same? Or would it look as old as my face? I took a deep breath and positioned the mirror between my legs. There it was. It looked exactly the same. A piece of skin stretched between my anus and vagina. I timidly touched my pinky to it. We were reunited. I started laughing and crying and shouting, "I HOPE YOU'RE WATCHING THIS, MOTHER! I'M PLAYING WITH MY TAINT! AND YOU CAN'T DO ANYTHING ABOUT IT. BECAUSE YOU'RE DEAD!"

(Audience claps.)

My taint was the opposite of dead. It was resurrected.
My taint is tiny. It's special. But most of all: it's mine.

(Thunderous applause.)

Taint-natrix

I came into this world taint first.

(Audience cheers.)

They call it a taint. Because it ain't the asshole, and it ain't the balls and it ain't the pussy. Taint nothin' there. Except a gorgeous delicious bite-size taint. Mmmmmmmm. I could go for some taint right now. I survive on it. It's how I make my living.

I'm what I call a taint-natrix. I specialize in the taint. People pay me good money to take care of their taint.

I will pierce your taint, paint your taint, burn your taint, ice your taint, slap your taint, blackmail your taint, whatever I feel like. I might even eat Thanksgiving dinner off your taint. And you better hold real still. Because if one dollop of stuffing falls into your asshole, I will literally eat your taint. And yours won't be the first taint I have shat out. Literally.

I didn't always dominate taints for a living. I used to be an architect. Worked for a prestigious firm. Designed several skyscrapers. Some of them famous. But then I took a trip to India and saw the Taj Mahal and I gave it all up. Someone had already built the most beautiful structure on the planet. A reflective pool separating mausoleums. A classic Indian interpretation of a taint. Maybe Emperor Shah Jahan's wife's taint. I can see her gorgeous watery taint now. No wonder he built that shit for her. I flew back home and threw my blueprints away. From then on out I was going to follow my passion: taints.

(Audience elated.)

Some of my customers are nervous at first.

Until I show them the taint within their taint. That's the secret. There's a tiny heartbeat in the center of a taint. Like a little mouse with no face or legs, just a heart. Bum-bum. Bum-bum. Bum-bum. And I have them touch their finger to the taint until they feel it and they are one with it. Bum-bum. Bum-bum. Everyone put their finger on their taint and find that mouse heart.

(Audience is quiet.)

DO IT! OR I WILL RIP OFF EVERYONE'S TAINT IN THE FRONT ROW!

(Uncomfortable laughing and movement.)

Very good. Now everyone shut your mouth holes and listen to your taint hearts.

Bum-bum. Feel it? Bum-bum. Say it with me!

("Bum-bum. Bum-bum.")

It's alive, ladies and gentlemen. And it's time to tame your taint.

(Sparse claps, due to one hand being indisposed.)

Old Taint

I'm sorry, I'm a little confused, what are we talking about today? My what? My saint? Well, I'm not Catholic, I'm afraid, but I do believe that my dog Bailey might be a saint reincarnated.

(Audience laughs.)

Oh no? Well, you'll have to forgive me. I'm eighty-eight years old. I got all my wits about me, I just don't hear too good sometimes. My what again? My taint. Why, what on earth? What's a taint? Oh, you have a diagram. Let me get my glasses.

(Puts on bifocals and stares at "diagram" on the fourth wall.)

Okay, what have we got here? There's the coochy-coo. Uh-huh, and that's where I make night soil.

(Audience giggles.)

So where's this taint? Right there? In the middle? Oh no, that's not the taint! That's the twixt!

(Audience gasps.)

That's right, at least the twixt is what we called it in my day. Because it was betwixt our Victory Gardens and our Kraut Holes.

(Audience listens, awestruck.)

Things were very different in my day. People weren't afraid of their twixts like they are now. When we would go on dates, we would kiss goodnight and then twixt-touch. And then if you really liked the guy, you would let him lick your boobs. But only if you approved of the way he touched your twixt.

The twixt was the real key to a lover's heart. If he touched it too soft, it probably meant he had a small prick. If he touched it too hard, he was obviously a dumb prick. Twixt-touching was a science!

It was the same for the gent. Based on a gal's timidity whilst touching his twixt he could measure how many men she had been with. Then it'd be clear if he was in the market for fresh snow or hot lava!

Now I was a lava girl myself. Mainly because I enjoyed the twixt-touch so much!

(Audience applause.)

Oh yes. I would have hundreds of men's fingerprints on my twixt. And a few women's too.

(One loud female yelp.)

These days I don't have anyone touching my twixt.

("I'll touch it!")

Oh! Ha, ha, thank you. No, no, the reason no one's touching my twixt is that I no longer have one anymore.

(Audience gasps.)

Yes. My twixt got very sick. Cancer. Had to take it out. That's what the doctor said. Well, actually, as I recall he did indeed say he was going to remove my "taint." And up until now I didn't know what that word referred to. I just remember waking up in the hospital with no twixt.

(A few sobs.)

Now, now, don't be sad for me! I still have my twixt! I had them save it for me and now I wear it around my neck, see?

(She pulls out a piece of flesh in a small glass bottle hanging off some leather string around her neck.)

No way was I going to let them take it away from me completely! It's my twixt! The world will keep changing, and whether it's your twixt then or your taint now, it will always be a special part of you.

(Audience claps.)

Impotence

It's the end of what has quite possibly been the most romantic day of your life. Breakfast in bed, then swimming with dolphins, followed by a spontaneous campfire on the beach and running home in the rain. Now you're giggling like schoolgirls and stripping out of wet clothes that still smell vaguely of dolphin hugs. Suddenly, your lover looks at you with hungry eyes. What happens next could very well be the greatest sexual experience you'll ever share with another soul, the perfect end to the perfect day.

*If you fail to get an erection, **pouting like a little baby** will only remind her of what you're incapable of giving her.*

But something's not right. For some reason, your penis isn't becoming erect. Rub it, lick it, suck it, stroke it, blow on it, and plead with it all you want; it just hangs there like a guilty child too ashamed to look you in the eye. What the hell is wrong with you? Unless that rain was whiskey and some of it accidentally splashed into your mouth, the problem is you're impotent.

Also known as **erectile dysfunction (ED)**, impotence affects an estimated 5 percent of men over 40, 20 percent of men over 65, and a whopping 100 percent of men over 120. But don't let the fact that you're not alone provide any assurance that being impotent is "okay." It's not. Having no dick whatsoever is preferable to the silly, sagging reminder of inadequacy that is a nonfunctioning penis. Nonetheless, impotent men typically seek treatment before grabbing a pair of garden shears and doing the honorable thing, so here are some facts:

The latest medical research has identified three leading causes or "excuses" for erectile dysfunction. They are:

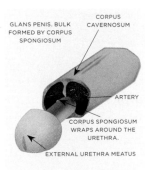

*The **anatomy of the penis** is something impotence sufferers probably shouldn't think about.*

- Psychological causes (e.g., stress, depression, low self-esteem, vaginaphobia)

- Physical problems (nerve damage, hole in side of penis that spurts blood when aroused, general wear and tear)

- Gypsy curses

The good news is, unless you've recently angered a gypsy, your penile affliction can be treated. That's because for one reason or another, erectile dysfunction has captivated the best and brightest minds of our male-dominated medical establishment, who in turn have produced no less than four clinically approved remedies for impotence.

IMPOTENCE DRUGS:

Medications like Viagra, Cialis, and Levitra work by increasing blood flow to the penis, but sometimes result in **priapism**, an erection lasting four hours or more (or, if you prefer, 240 one-minute erections all in a row). Left untreated, priapism can damage erectile tissue and result in a permanent loss of function, making these drugs the equivalent of a highly effective cold remedy that might make your nose dry up and fall off your face.

VACUUM CONSTRICTION DEVICES (VCDS):

These are ordinary penis pumps, modified to cost your health insurance provider $500. VCDs use suction to draw blood into the penis and imprison it there against its will with a constricting band or ring. Unfortunately, a vacuum-induced erection is not the same as a natural one and tends to be purplish, numb, and cold, which is ideal for any woman who enjoys being fucked by a sad grape Popsicle.

PENILE IMPLANT:

An affront to nature that demonstrates the indignities men will suffer to keep getting boners, this surgically-implanted monstrosity incorporates tubing, fluid, and a hidden squeeze pump in order to achieve erection. The wealthy old man's penis of tomorrow, using the sneaker technology of the 1990s.

STRAPPING YOUR PENIS TO A DILDO:

Not ideal, but better than no sex at all.

If none of these treatments work, you'll just have to tell your partner the bad news: that "deer" you hit a few weeks ago with your Land Rover must have been a gypsy, and now your penis is cursed. Hopefully, she'll be so impressed that you drive a Rover, she just might forget about your "condition." (Not likely.)

Just the Tip!

Impotence is often an indicator of more serious health problems, such as diabetes, high cholesterol, and Parkinson's disease. So don't worry—you might not have to live with impotence much longer!

FLACCIDOPOLY

The Game of Engorgement

WHAT YOU'LL NEED:

- Dice
- A game piece representing your inability to perform as a man (wet noodle, a thimble of tears)
- A penis

HOW TO PLAY:

Place your game piece on START. Take deep, relaxing breaths and roll the die, clearing your mind of any stressful thoughts. Move your game piece the number of spaces indicated. Follow the instructions on each space. Most important, try not to worry. If you don't win, you can always try again later (though you should probably just give up and watch a movie).

Droopy Drawer

GET OUT OF BED FREE.

THIS CARD MAY BE KEPT U[...] MANHOOD IS RESTORED.

Droopy Drawer

PHARMACEUTICAL COMPANY CHOOSES YOU FOR EXPERIMENTAL IMPOTENCE DRUG TRIAL. COLLECT $500

Boner

WAITRESS SNICKERS WHEN YOU ORDER "SOFT NOODLES."

PAY HUMILIATION TAX $45

Droopy Drawer

PAY IMPOTENCE TAX $15.

Boner

LADYFRIEND CAN'T HIDE HER TEARS OF DISAPPOINTMENT.

COLLECT TRAUMATIC EXPERIENCE INSURANCE $100

FLACCIDOPOLY

GO BACK 2

penis

wait, there was a breeze on your

You're cured! Oh

Congratulations,

FULLY ERECT

ROLL AGAIN

it now

suck if you lost

much it would

think about how

there! Try not to

You're almost

GO BACK 2

constrictor

like latex boa

Condom feels

Managed to cram yourself into a rubber

MOVE AHEAD 1

Can't help but imagine your partner telling all his/her friends about your pathetic, doughy manhood

GO BACK 1

START

Manage to stop crying

MOVE AHEAD 1

Dog ate your boner pills

GO BACK

A few blood cells accidentally wander into your penis

MOVE AHEAD 2

Just remembered you didn't pay the cable bill

GO BACK 2

Poking the Peanut

If you are infected with a sexually transmitted baby, your life is about to change drastically. You have to be mindful of what you eat, what you drink, and most important, whom you have sex with. Because like it or not, you're having sex for two now. Here are some chilling firsthand accounts from former fetuses traumatized by their time in the womb.

JIM

"Even though it was a long time ago I still have nightmares. A worm trying to get me. Or at least tapping me on the shoulder to get my attention. I try to get away but I'm trapped, tied there by a tube. Worst of all, I don't have arms to slap it away. Needless to say, I'm not big on fishing or gardening."

EAMON

"I remember like it was yesterday. I was just chewing on placenta, minding my own business, when all of a sudden I heard my mom moaning. I was scared because I'd never heard those sounds before, just Beethoven. Not this spooky moaning business. And then my whole world started rocking up and down real fast, like an earthquake. I thought I was going to die. Then things went back to normal, and I ate some more placenta."

JANEANE

"My mom was really into vibrators. At least once a day I'd hear the buzz and everything around me would vibrate. It would last for 30 minutes to an hour, which in the dark seems like an eternity. At first I liked it. It broke up the monotony. But once my bones developed they started to rattle together, and that was annoying."

MARVE! HOLY SHIT! YOU'RE A SQUIRTER!

IT WAS HER FIRST ORGASM WITH HER FIRST LOVE. SHE WAS A SQUIRTER, A WOMAN WHO CAN EJACULATE FASTER AND HARDER THAN A MAN, ONLY MARVELENE'S SEX JUICES WERE LETHAL.

SHE FLED THAT NIGHT. AND DID THE ONLY THING SHE COULD: FIGHT CRIME WITH HER DEADLY VAGINA WATER. SHE IS...

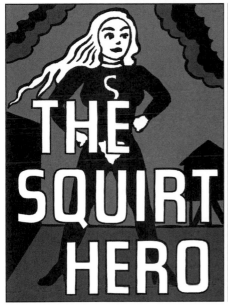

THE SQUIRT HERO

SHE WAS THE PERFECT CRIME FIGHTER— CRIMINALS NEVER SUSPECTED HER POWERS. SHE COULD FINISH A JOB IN SECONDS.

WHEN THE POLICE FINALLY ARRIVED ON THE SCENE THE WICKED WRETCHES WERE MELTED AND THE SURVIVORS WERE TOO TURNED ON TO SPEAK.

SOMETHING TO BE SAID ABOUT HAVING A FEROCIOUS VAG AND BANGING TITS— PEOPLE FORGET TO LOOK YOU IN THE EYE.

DAILY PROBING-EXAMINER
SQUIRT HERO'S IDENTITY REMAINS UNKNOWN

UNFORTUNATELY FOR THE SLIME ON THE STREET, NOTHING GOT MARVELENE'S ROCKS OFF MORE THAN CRIME.

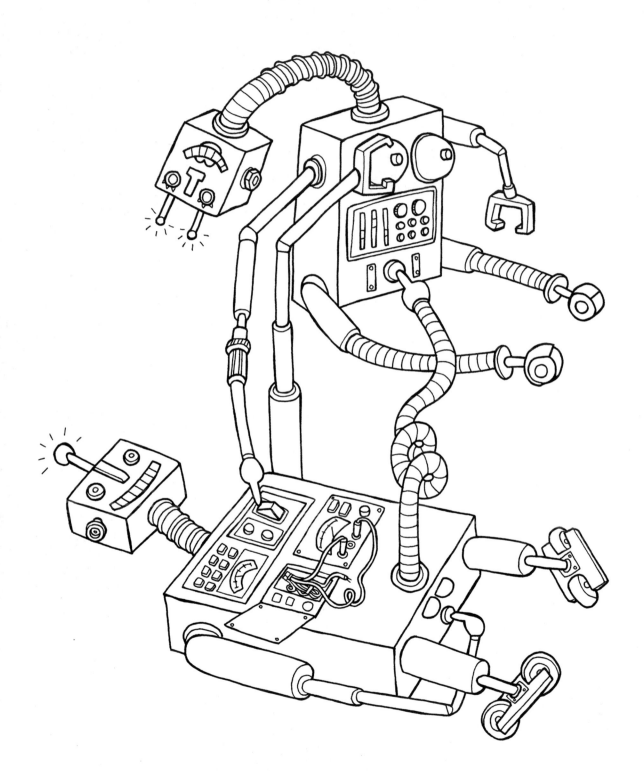

The Future of Sex

THE FUTURE IS COMING

Can you read this? If not, it's probably because your primitive organic eyes can't yet process the super-advanced hyperfonts of 6969. Look away! BEFORE YOUR EYES EXPLODE AND YOU GET PRIMITIVE EYE JUICE ALL OVER THIS ELECTRO-PAPER.

But not being able to decipher cool twelfth-dimensional typography like Space-Times New Roman and Cosmic Sans is the least of your problems. Because if you can't read this, it means your sexual consciousness is trapped in a carbon-based blood suitcase of a body, forced to have intercourse by "touching."

Eww.

That kind of crude, juvenile sex seems almost comical in the year 6969. To put it in hyperspeak:

```
10 PRINT "YOUR SEX IS BORING AND INEFFICIENT"

20 GOTO 10

RUN
```

Sorry, that was harsh. But come on! Did it honestly never occur to you that the world would be a much happier place if your leaders were hermaphrodites? Or that you could clone spare bodies in case you get an STD? Were you even trying to be sexy? Don't bother answering, because I don't care. Get ready for the briefest of glimpses into a whole new universe of sexual delights and wonders you'll never get to experience, because you'll be dead. Oh no. What's that coming out of your eyes? Is that . . . eye juice? Watch it, you clumsy oaf! If you get any of that primitive fluid on the electro-paper you'll—

Dear God. What have you done? You've shorted out my hyperformatting! You've got to help me before my kerning matrix ruptures or I'll be stuck forever in Zaph xb c v F H S B Y H W A J B S Y J K D S

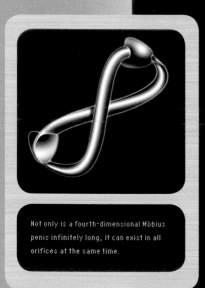

Not only is a fourth-dimensional Möbius penis infinitely long, it can exist in all orifices at the same time.

Teledildonics

In the future, you'll be having the best sex of your life, and your partner won't even be there. No, you won't be masturbating (at least not every time). You'll be fucking each other thousands of miles apart with the help of remote stimulation devices known as **teledildos**.

A technology still in its infancy, teledildonics combines the latest advances in communication with the crude vibrating, sucking, and "massaging" mechanisms we've used in sex toys for the past hundred years. The result: no longer is your distance from your lover during sex limited to the length of the penis. Now, you can be literally millions of penises away and still fuck each other's brains out—just don't expect any cuddling afterward.

What does it all mean? It means that in the future, the dorky kid who claims to have a girlfriend in Canada may not only be telling the truth, but also getting more action than you, teledildonically.

Teledildonic devices will likely be stored in a robonightstand.

Here are just a few forms this genital-exciting new technology could take:

oPHONES

Let's face it: so-called phone sex isn't sex. It's masturbating with a phone in your hand. And if your phone-a-friend-with-benefits isn't good at talking dirty, you're tempted to call 911 and report a violent crime: your genitals being bored to death.

Thankfully, teledildonic telephones, or **dildophones**, will change all that. Featuring either a penile antenna or a vaginal input port, these kinky communicators will boast a vibrate mode five hundred times more powerful than anything on the market today. Meaning that your future lover may be whispering sweet nothings, but you'll definitely be feeling some sweet somethings . . . and they will rattle your astro-fillings with ecstasy.

Yet for all its promise, dildophone technology faces three major obstacles:

 Dropped calls could result in blue balls.

 It's likely you'd get annoying unsolicited orgasms from teledildomarketers (probably during dinner).

 Sitting on your phone and accidentally dialing your parents would technically constitute incest.

Are oPhones basically vibrators? How dare you! They are *vibrating phones you hold against your crotch*, something only imaginable in the future.

ROBOSEXTING

It's the future and you're relaxing, reading the cyberpaper in front of a roaring gamma fire. It's another quiet night at home. You've had a lot of them lately with your girlfriend out of the galaxy shooting that big-budget holomovie with George Cloney.*

Suddenly, there's a knock on the portal. You open it to find a sexy robot, looking more or less like the lover for whom you've been pining. Before you can say a word, it shoots laser beams out of its eyes and vaporizes your technozipper. As your futuristic silver pants fall to the floor, the unannounced android's mouth begins to glow with a soothing orange light. Then, with passionate metal eyes, the machine lurches toward your—

Programming a robosexter

This is the basic concept behind the remote-controlled sex machines of the future known as robosexters. The term is based on "sexting," the early twenty-first-century practice of using mobile phones to send regrettable photos and declarations of horniness to future ex-boyfriends. Robosexting expands on this notion, only instead of blurry shots of your initials shaved into some crazy girl's pubic hair, it's a sexy metal messenger that's traveled thousands of miles to deliver the orgasms your partner couldn't give in person.

A robosexter's program determines exactly how it goes about doing this. Early versions might let users string together routines of preprogrammed sex acts (e.g., LAP DANCE, HAND JOB, HEART-SHAPED HICKEY, REPEAT), while advanced models will allow for more personalized messages (e.g., that "thing" you do with your "thing"). This level of detail will require "teaching" the robot with a motion-capture suit, or possibly just fucking it the way you want it to fuck. This, however, is dangerous territory, given that there's no quicker way to make a robot fall in love with you.

---

* After his death, actor George Clooney will be cloned using the copious amounts of leftover DNA in his bedroom. The result of this experiment and all subsequent dashing replicas will be named "George Cloney."

The thrill is not knowing who's on the other side of space-time.

GLORY WORMHOLES

No matter how lifelike robosexters become, in the end you'd still be settling for a bucket of bolts that may or may not be secretly planning to murder you and steal your lover. The ideal teledildonic would let you actually be there, cutting the jealous robot out of the equation and allowing you to get some faraway poonanny in the flesh. This is the thrilling concept behind glory wormholes. A glory wormhole is a hypothetical phenomenon that provides a shortcut to a distant part of the universe, but is only big enough to accommodate something the size of a penis (even then posing a significant risk of time-splinters). Sound crazy? That's because it is crazy. It's sticking your cock into a rift in the space-time continuum and hoping someone or something a million light years away will give you a hummer.

From a teledildonic standpoint, the first impulse might be to somehow manipulate glory wormholes so you could control where they go. But even if this were possible, would it really be the most exciting way to use them? Your penis could travel to the farthest reaches of the known universe, experiencing pleasures not yet conceived of by our primitive human brains. Even if there were nothing on the other side, the vacuum of space would put any penis pump to shame. Knowing all this, would you still want to bother your out-of-town girlfriend with a disembodied, intergalactic hard-on right in the middle of her big business presentation? Probably not.

As if the prospects weren't already exciting enough, glory wormholes could also let your penis travel through time. By accelerating your end of a wormhole to a velocity approaching the speed of light, anything that entered (e.g., your penis) would exit at a point in time prior to its entry. Meaning, at least in theory, you could get a blow job from Marilyn Monroe, Cleopatra, Hitler's mom, or even a younger version of yourself (assuming you cruised glory wormholes during your "experimental phase").

Yet for all the mysteries of glory wormholes, one thing is certain: if they do exist, they make for some very happy worms.

STDs 2.0:
Standard Tomorrow Diseases

Though we can hope for a future when STDs are eradicated, that probably won't be the case. Viral mutations and what appears to be a spreading epidemic of bass players with latex allergies will mean a whole new generation of super STDs. Of course there's no way of knowing exactly what these groin-spoiling nightmares will do to us, but it makes for fun/terrifying speculation.

COMPUTER CLAP

First spread from laptop computers to actual laps, this highly contagious STD will be the first computer virus to make the leap to nonmechanical hosts. (Future rumor has it some sicko fucked his MacBook.) With even "clean-looking" Web sites capable of spreading the virus, masturbating to Internet porn will no longer be safe sex. Computer clap will be able to sneak past any antivirus program, meaning the only firewall you'll care about is the one that activates when you pee.

GLOW CROTCH

One of the worst things about STDs is the stigma, especially when it comes in the form of a ridiculous glowing wang visible through five pairs of underwear. Unfortunately, that's exactly what happens with glow crotch, a clingy phosphorescent bacterium that turns shame into shine. The more embarrassed you get, the brighter it becomes. Which means for glow crotch sufferers (also known as **beacon britches**), going to a movie, the planetarium, or any other first date that doesn't take place in near-blinding sunlight will probably be your last. Worst of all: the laughter ringing in your ears anytime someone tells you to "look on the bright side."

DEATHBED BUGS

As STDs go, deathbed bugs won't be all that bad. Most carriers will spend their whole lives oblivious to these internal parasites that don't eat much and rarely throw parties. But when deathbed bugs realize the gravy train is pulling into Heaven Station, they'll FREAK THE FUCK OUT. Bursting from the abdomen of their dying host, the dramatic exit of deathbed bugs will ruin many a touching farewell with a creepy-crawly reminder of Grandma's "wild days."

THE TORCH

The arrival of aliens to Earth will introduce our first mental STD. Nicknamed "the torch," this affliction stems from the crippling emotional letdown that follows hooking up with a sexually advanced being. After all, if aliens are sophisticated enough to travel millions of light-years, they're going to be dynamite in the sleep pod. How can you not be depressed when it's over? Fortunately, there is a cure. All the pain, all the loneliness . . . it would all go away if Glryyynxtswx would just come back, if only for a little bit. Maybe if you made him a really impressive crop circle in the backyard, he'd drop by and say hi. It certainly couldn't hurt . . . (Besides, you don't really like corn anyway.)

Our Future Bodies

It's often said that the body is a temple. But if you knew a "carpenter" who could get his hands on some cheap "lumber" from a dead "tree," slapping on a few additions wouldn't be disrespecting the temple—it would be increasing the property value! Fortunately, this will be a common scenario in a future rich in medical waste and day laborers with cosmetic surgery experience.

Assuming current trends in body improvement hold firm (probably a little too firm), this is what we'll be doing to ourselves in the future.

	BEFORE	AFTER	AFTERER
STOMACH	Well-fed	Chiseled	Gilled
BOOBS	Who cares? They're boobs!	Spherical	Multi-nippled
LIPS	Painted	Plumped	Duck-billed
ANUS	Worm-free	Bleached	Bejeweled
BODY (MEN)	Intermittently hairy	Bronzed	Titaniumed
BODY (WOMEN)	Hourglass	Minuteglass	Levitating torso

Braingasms:
Get Ready to Have Your Mind Blown (Literally)

Despite its squishy texture, unappealing gray color, and sickening association with open head wounds, the brain is the sexiest part of the human body. Sure, you tend to think of your tingling, throbbing, engorging, and all-around naughtier "lower bits" as the sexy ones, but behind the scenes, it's your brain that's pulling the pleasure strings and turning the tiny crank that makes your toes curl. Pretty sexy, brain.

Given the brain's role in achieving orgasm, it's only a matter of time before people start fucking with it, in all senses of the word. By stimulating specific areas of the brain with electricity, chemicals, or teensy-weensy glasses of champagne, we could give our lovers and ourselves the longest, most powerful orgasms in history. As if that weren't incentive enough,

brain sex would also let us bypass our malfunction-prone (and let's face it, silly-looking) genitals. Gone would be the days of fiddling with tricky clitorises and waiting for penises to reboot. Suddenly, "pressing our buttons" would be as easy as flipping a switch, or perhaps pulling a lever of some kind.*

Unfortunately, one side effect of cutting out the middle organ is that there's no going back. With every generation, our neglected genitals would atrophy, until they finally lost all function. And though our head-rattling orgasms would more than make up for the indignity of being hung like a pygmy, deep down inside we'd know we'd destroyed something beautiful. We would, in a very real sense, have **creamed our genes**.

That's not to say *everything* would shrink. Given the brain's affinity for reward, the areas associated with orgasm would likely expand in an evolutionary effort to accept greater and greater stimulation. Over time, the sexification of our gray matter would not only change the shape of the brain, but the skull that encases it. And you can bet those swinging the most brain-pipe will walk with a certain swagger . . . and not just because they don't have to worry about squishing their microscopic testicles between their thighs.

*A man with a **sexually advanced brain**.*

* Oh, or a *button!* Duh.

As with every new technology, there will be those who abuse it. For the lazy and unemployed, the temptation will be to spend all day in bed "floggin' the noggin" (see inset). Even scarier, should our brain circuitry be hacked as easily as our computers, we would face the daunting possibility of losing control of our orgasms. Sure, the first couple of times your buddies made you climax in the food court it would be hilarious. But it would get annoying . . . fast. Just imagine a world where you had an uncontrollable orgasm every time you saw a Big Mac. Are you picturing it? Well, enjoy it. Because once McDonald's gets their hands on your brain codes, you won't be able to imagine anything without being interrupted by an unsolicited McOrgasm.

Of course, exhausted brain-havers will try fortifying their craniums with orgasm-blocking software, but ultimately, people will give in to the ecstasy onslaught. Why? Because we'll want to give in. After all, they're FREE ORGASMS. And in the end, humans will come to cherish the rare moments of not cumming that will be known as **blandmaxing**.

The Sexy Book of Sexy Sex's

TOP FIVE FUTURE NICKNAMES FOR BRAIN-MASTURBATING

DRAINING THE BRAIN

CANOODLING THE NOODLE

STROKING THE IMAGINATION

SNAPPING THE SYNAPSES

MEDULLAING THE OBLONGATA

Sex Guides of the Future

In the future, thumbing through pages of compressed wood pulp to learn about sex will seem just as primitive and silly as stuffing untrustworthy penises into latex bags. Here are just a few of the ways in which future sexperts will learn their trade:

The Sexy Pill of Sexy Sex

The ultimate compendium of sexual knowledge in convenient pill form. Do not take while operating heavy machinery or risk losing virginity to a backhoe.

The Sexy Ride of Sexy Sex

Sex can be an emotional rollercoaster. So why not learn about it on one? This educational thrill ride will make you scream one way or another. Like all good sexual encounters, be prepared to wait in line.

The Sexy Suppository of Sexy Sex

All the benefits of the Sexy Pill of Sexy Sex without having to track down a glass of water. Great for babies and pets. Not so great for chili cook-offs.

"THE GAZELLEMO AFFAIR"

Nothing is more annoying than having to slice a throat in an antigravity chamber. Blood floats everywhere like a snow globe from hell. When you rotate the dial back to *g* you have to brace yourself for things to land where they may. You never commit a murder in a floater. It's impossible to hide the evidence. The only good thing is that a jury will know it's not premeditated. This was a crime of the heart.

It was 3010 when I signed up with the Marines to fight China. They printed my name wrong on my anti-incinerating vest: Jesse Bain, instead of Jessie, the spelling for girls. I don't fault them, I'm as androgynous as they come, and it would be another year till I sprouted milk mounds. In the battle zone, people couldn't tell if I had balls or was just crazy. Watching me test Chinese vapor shields without my prosthetics was thrilling at first, and then it just became bad for morale. The officers pulled me off combat. My new assignment was to dig a secret hole connecting China and the States. I got an acid blaster, a portable cipher drill, and some alone time. Five days later I was lost in Pakistan. I should have dug east. Never did have a good sense of direction.

In Pakistan I got myself straightened out. On the outskirts of Karachi they were trafficking gazellemos. I traded my digging equipment and a few privileged military secrets for five gazellemos and transportation back to New York. I knew I had come out on top in the deal. For the first time I was excited about living.

Gazellemos are half gazelle, half human. Fifty years ago a lonely deviant successfully mated with a domesticated gazelle and out came a gazellemo. As soon as that baby freak was spotted in public the world became obsessed with gazellemos. People were fornicating with poor gazelles left and right. Before long a tiny population emerged. I have to admit, I'm no kinky creeptard, but they are stunning to look at. Their human ears and twisting horns frame enormous eyes. Long, elegant cheekbones connect their snouts. Walking upright, they are completely covered in shimmering caramel body hair with a striking black stripe down their sides. Their feet and hands are the only unsightly thing on them. It's like they couldn't figure out whether to be hands or hooves so they came out as stubs, or halves as we call them. But no one notices the halves. Their esoteric beauty exudes an exotic sexiness. Which is why they're so illegal.

It took awhile for the powers that be to realize that the root of all evil wasn't money any longer—it was sex. And they did a bang-up job of putting a lid on it. Now we reproduce like fish. Eggs are dropped in a lab and sprinkled with sperm a few days later. Pregnancy is illegal, unsafe, and discriminatory. All people and genders must be equal. Babies grow in tutoring incubators. By the time they can breathe on their own they're fluent in two languages and have a sixteenth-grade reading level. People don't hook up, they don't watch porn, and they definitely don't masturbate. All of those things are punishable by life-passing. But the government doesn't want to be inhumane, so before you come out of the incubator a vibrating chip is planted in your genitals. It goes off once a day as long as your heart keeps beating. Everyone is given a different time so the entire world doesn't pause together for an orgasm break. Mine happens at 4 AM. Which blows because I never get a full night's sleep. But at least I'm always alone.

The government's strategy has paid off. People cling to their work for stimulation. The only desire left is for productivity. Anything with a hint of sex is terminated. Entertainment is a thing of the past. Sleep and dunks are our only escape. When the gazellemos came on the scene they were a bigger threat than China. They were banned from the U.S., and exterminated. But that didn't stop people from wanting them.

So I decided I would supply for the demand. I hid my gazelle-mos in textile orbs and successfully smuggled them to my dunk in Hell's Kitchen. My dunk was next to Hudson Field. After the river dried up the soil was rich enough to harvest potatoes. That's all we eat now. Dried riverbeds are the only land left for crops, and potatoes are the one vegetation that can survive the polluted atmosphere. The potato pickers come to my dunk after work for moonsheen. Some of the pickers are old enough to remember when there was whiskey. I wish they'd shut up about it. If I ever turn into a geezer drinking dunk slosh and bitching about it, I'll know to end it with a scythe pen. I keep one coded to my inner thigh.

The basement of the dunk used to be an ancient strip club. Since stripping was outlawed the place was worthless and my mother figure, or MF, bought it on the cheap. MF and I found a surveillance hologram recorder hidden behind a booth, and we watched how they used to strip. It was beautiful. Back in the day the females had large milk mounds and looked really feminine. Today there are only a few subtle characteristics separating men and women's appearances. My MF might as well be a FF, it wouldn't matter. The sexes have identical roles. The only benefit of living with another woman is we can split a de-nesting cake in the mornings. Obliterates the uterus painlessly over time.

MF was unconscious in a plasma bed when I brought back the gazellemos. She had suffered from thin organs all her life, and she was steadily becoming transparent. We didn't make enough off moonsheen to get her into a floater. If she could at least sleep nights without the big *g* pulling on her tissues she would live past 120. But the way she was looking, throwing her a century party was going to take a miracle.

I needed to make some major ching off my gazellemos. I was nervous when I let my contraband out of their orbs. How was I going to teach them to strip when they couldn't master English or even Arabic? Turns out I had nothing to worry about. The French fry solved everything. The gazellemos were starving, and they learned fast for a treat. The hardest part was designing their magnetic outfits, since their clumsy halves can't work a hook or a zipper. In just a few days I had my secret gazellemo club up and running. And in one month, MF was waking up in a floater.

It's hard to know whom to trust when you become the wealthiest person in Hell's Kitchen. I had ching dripping out of my tunics. The word was out that I had the goods. My dunk was packed every night. At first it pissed the pickers off. What the hell were these ching-rollers from fancy-pants Queens doing in their dunk? But then I paid off a tomb curator to swipe some whiskey from an old life-passer's tomb. The pickers shut up for the first time in their lives. Their mouths were filled with sweet liquor. And they were right, that stuff's amazing.

I had to hire help. I needed a few bouncers to collect the ching, protect the gazellemos from overzealous patrons, and look out for busts. Solar was the first person I hired. He could pay off the cops for me because he used to be one. He looked like me, except broader and happier. His smile always got bigger when he got paid. And everyone was getting paid. Even the gazellemos, who couldn't leave the basement, were pampered.

I hired a personal fryer to crisp their potatoes. For a while I even bought five oversized tutoring incubators to see if they could learn language. But it was a waste. Their tongues were too long, and they would instantly fall asleep in the cube's warmth. My failed efforts to integrate them into modern society only confirmed my view of them as a commodity. They often tripped and fell on the stage due to their halves, but their gaze was intoxicating. They knew how to remove their costumes slowly. People would pay any price to see it. My gazellemos became more precious than hybrid crank. The price inflated to 65,000 chings for admission, for a one-hour show. A few cops became secret regulars. We didn't have to pay them off too much, as long as they got to touch the gazellemos.

MF became involved after seven months of being in her floater. She was more solid; her tissues had rejuvenated and were at least ten years younger. She had a memory of one or two talk songs that were around when she was younger, before music devolved into digital tone. She was able to replicate the sounds on an antique synthesizer. It brought the dunk down.

I began developing a bond with Solar that was new to me. Romance was a term I overheard a babbling cranked-up geezer mention, something about flowers and fingering. Not sure what a fingering is. But there was something between Solar and myself that transcended the daily interactions and ching transactions. We were living a life in defiance of the law. We were breaking rules ingrained in us since our conception, and there were certain body parts that were sounding off a rebel yell. Mainly my female tube. Every time Solar came around, the Hudson River flooded back to life under my tunic. At 4 AM my daily orgasm was now accompanied by a vision of Solar. I noticed Solar got his at 9 PM. I knew that because he would look at me right before he tore off his juice absorber.

But I didn't know what to do about it. To my knowledge there was no record of these emotions that I was having. It wasn't the desperate lusting that my audiences felt when they watched a gazellemo undress. There was an odd tenderness. I wanted to be around Solar all the time. I wanted to be him. It made me sick. It got so bad at one point I even put the scythe pen to my wrist. But the thought of never seeing Solar again stopped me. I needed to do something or I was going to lose my mind.

"Thanks for meeting me here early." The words fell out of me like broken radiation crystals. We were in MF's floater. It was the only place where we could be alone. MF was downstairs doing the gazellemos' hair for the show.

"What is it, Jessie? I hope I didn't do anything wrong." He was shaking. I immediately got rid of the gravity so it wouldn't be so noticeable.

"No, you've been great. I just felt there might be something we are not saying to each other." My palms were dripping, what was wrong with me? Solar looked even worse. He was as white as a comet parade. We were lighter than air, but the anxiety was weighing us down.

"Jessie, I've been very up-front with you about where the ching is going. Everyone in the precinct is covered." Why was he all business? That was the furthest thing from my mind. Frustrated by a lack of words, I started to pull off my tunic. I did it slowly like the ancient strippers and the gazellemos did it. I bobbed in the chamber with my exposed milk mounds pointing right at Solar. Now we were both speechless. Neither of us had any idea what to do.

Solar took off his tunic too. And then his juice absorber. I took off my shell sheath, and both of us removed our crocks. It was like we were back in the incubator again, but with no teacher. Solar's body was thin, revealing every vein and most of his organs. I couldn't stop staring at his male tube. He noticed and instantly covered it.

"It's hideous," he whispered. His embarrassment awoke an instinct in me to protect him. I pulled myself right in front of him and held his male tube.

"It's incredibly ugly. But I want to take care of it." I caressed it to show Solar that I wasn't repulsed by his male tube, and we were both surprised to see it take a different shape.

"It's bigger!" I looked at Solar in disbelief. Was he okay? Solar pressed it harder against my hands.

"It's aching!" He began to cry. I'd never seen this before, but I had a feeling it had something to do with romance. I needed to comfort him. I pushed his body against the side of the floater and pinned us together by holding onto some pegs. I wrapped my legs around his pelvis, and to my surprise I felt his male tube go right inside my female tube! We both gasped in fear and wonder. We froze for a few moments, afraid that if we moved something would break and this perfect fit would end. My sweaty grip failed, and I started floating backward. Solar grabbed me and pulled me back toward him. Our tubes were still joined. It felt wonderful. I let go again, sliding backward on his male tube, and he waited till the last second to pull me back. The sensation was so pleasurable. It felt natural. We started laughing like children. We continued to do this. The more we did it the better it felt. We went faster and faster till we felt our vibrating chips go off. But it wasn't our scheduled time. We stared at Solar's milky juice floating up between us. The absorber was useless now. I let go of Solar and we floated around each other, in awe of what just happened. I wanted to do it again. I wanted to seal the floater and do it forever. I understood instantly why this became illegal.

"I guess we should get back. But, um, that's all I wanted to say to you." I awkwardly fished for my tunic.

"Well, that's not what I expected. But it was perfect." We looked into each other's eyes and smiled. And it was at that moment that a government chip floated past my face. I grabbed it in disbelief. I pressed it to my forehead just as Solar lunged for it.

Insider: Solar Armstrong. Meeting: Tomorrow, 8 AM. With: President. Subject: Illegal Gazellemo Facility; Leaked Military Secrets. Payment: Government Position Plus Double Ching. Status: Highly Classified.

It was my turn to shake. With rage. Before Solar could think of a lie I had already decoded my scythe pen and pushed it through his neck. It was easy to go for a jugular so visible under translucent skin. Before I pulled my pen out I paused to watch the life go out of his eyes. On the one hand I regretted destroying the person who made me feel something new. But on the other, I was feeling more like myself.

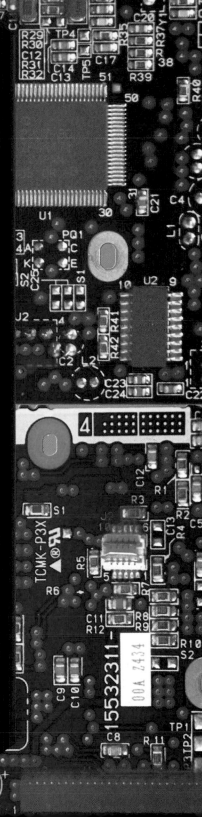

Photo Credits

Chapter 1

6: Author photo: **Gretchen LeMaistre. 14:** Pony: **Duncan Hull. 15:** Hammerhead sharks: **Kathy Wynn: DT**. Komodo dragon: **Nicholas Hinks.** Snail: **Petr Kovar.** Aphids: **R. Grabe. 17:** Firefly: **Cathy Keifer: DT**. Grasshopper: **John Boyer.** Elephant Seal: **Luis Rock.** Saudi shiek: **Creative-marc: DT**. Salmon: **Dieter K. Henke: IS**. Raver: **Nicole S. Young: IS**. Men on Street: **Peeter Viisimaa: IS**. Bowerbird: **Nickolay Stanev: DT**. Squid: **Wksp: DT**. Michael Phelps, Sting, Martha Stewart: **AP. 18:** Mudshark: **Greg Ampstman: DT. 20:** Bonobo Monkey, **Michelle White: DT. 21:** Pigeon: **Joachim Bär.**

Chapter 2

25: *The Creation of Adam,* **Michelangelo Buonarroti**; Vatican Museums and Galleries, Vatican City, Italy; *Adam and Eve,* **J. Urseline**: Private Collection: Photo © Bonhams, London, UK: **BAL. 26:** *Venus of Willendorf:* Naturhistorisches Museum, Vienna, Austria : **BAL.** Kinkaku-ji Kyoto: **Attila Jandi: DT. 28:** *Portrait of Lorenzo de' Medici 'the Magnificent':* Palazzo Medici-Riccardi, Florence, Italy: **BAL.** *Vitruvian man:* **IS**. Bonnie and Clyde: **AP. 29:** Rosie the Riveter, AIDs quilt, Robert Pattinson: **AP. 36:** *Giacomo Casanova,* **Ismael Mengs**: Private Collection: Archives Charmet; *Portrait of the Marquis de Sade Surrounded by Devils:* Private Collection: **BAL.** *Cleopatra:* **IS. 37:** *Catherine the Great,* **Johann Baptist Lampi**; Hermitage, St. Petersburg, Russia; *Portrait of Emily Dickinson (1830-86) as a Child:* Private Collection: **BAL.** Liberace: **AP. 38:** Wilt Chamberlain, Madonna: **AP.**

Chapter 3

55: Cactus: **IS.**

Chapter 4

65: *Noah and the Dove,* **Clive Uptton**: Private Collection: © Look and Learn: **BAL.**

Chapter 5

96-97: Background: **Basslinegfx: DT.**

Chapter 6

108: President Buchanan: **LOC.**

114: Nadya Suleman, Bobsled: **AP.** Scarlet Macaw: **Kurt Raihn.** Barbados beach: **Gregory Runyan. 115:** Sphinx: **Samantha Villagran.** Taj Mahal: **V Satya Ramachandran.** Taliban soldier, Kim Jong Il: **AP.**

Chapter 7

126: Hermaphroditus: **Marie-Lan Nguyen. 127:** Playing Card Art: **Roberto1977: DT. 129:** Boston Corbett: **LOC. 130:** *The Triumph of Pan,* Nicolas Poussin: Louvre, Paris, France / Giraudon **BAL. 131:** Statue of Dionysus: **IS.**

Chapter 8

151: AIDS virus: **IS. 152:** *Self Portrait with Felt Hat,* **Vincent van Gogh**: Van Gogh Museum, Amsterdam, The Netherlands: **BAL.** Henry the VIII: **IS. 153:** Knight: **IS.** Eva Peron, Bigfoot, **AP.** Hepatitis B: **Woodooart: IS. 154:** Car: **Andrew Beierle.** Prostitute: **IS. 162:** Sulking man: **Redbaron: DT.**

Chapter 9

173: Bedroom Background: **Neha Agrawal: DT.**

Key

AP: AP Images
BAL: The Bridgeman Art Library
DT: Dreamstime.com
IS: iStockphoto.com
LOC: Library of Congress

Illustration credits:

Chapter opener illustrations: **12, 22, 46, 62, 80, 106, 122, 148, 170;** Wildo's Retreat, **132-133:** © Lisa Hanawalt.

Illustrations: **21, 27, 28, 30-31, 32, 69, 70-71, 94-95, 109-110, 134-135, 140-141, 154, 155, 156, 164-165, 167-169, 174, 176-177, 179:** © Michael Kupperman.

Augmentooming, **50:** © Oguz Aral: **IS.**

Trademarks

Abercrombie® is a registered trademark of Abercrombie & Fitch Co. Atari® is a registered trademark of Infogrames, Inc. Banana Republic® is a registered trademark of Banana Republic (Apparel), LLC. Band-Aid® is a registered trademark of Johnson and Johnson. Big Mac® is a registered trademark of McDonald's Corporation. Botox® Cosmetic is a registered trademark owned by Allergan. British Sterling® is a registered trademark of Dana. Cialis® is a registered trademark of Eli Lilly ICOS, LLC. Coke® is a registered trademark of The Coca-Cola Company. Corvette® is a registered trademark of the General Motors Corporation. Craigslist® is a registered trademark of Craigslist. Crisco® is a registered trademark of the J.M. Smucker Company. Dictaphone® is a registered trademark of Dictaphone Corp. Dixie® is a registered trademark of James River Corporation. Filet-O-Fish® is a registered trademark of McDonald's Corporation. Gap® is a registered trademark of Gap (Apparel), LLC. Glock® is a registered trademark of Glock, Ges m.b.H. Head & Shoulders® is a registered trademark of Procter & Gamble. Jacuzzi® is a registered trademark of Jacuzzi Inc. Jenga® is a registered trademark of Pokonobe Associates. Kellogg® is a registered trademark of the Kellogg Company. KFC® is a registered trademark of KFC Corporation. Land Rover® is a registered trademark of Land Rover North America, Inc. Levitra® is a registered trademark of Bayer Aktiengesellschaft and is used under license by GlaxoSmithKline and Schering Corporation. MacBook® is a registered trademark of Apple Inc. McDonald's® is a registered trademark of McDonald's Corporation. Moog® is a registered trademark of Moog Inc. Nutella® is a registered trademark of Ferrero Spa. Old Navy® is a registered trademark of Old Navy (Apparel), LLC. Pop Rocks® is a registered trademark of owned by Zeta Espacial S.A. and is distributed by Pop Rocks, Inc. Popsicle® is a registered trademark of Unilever. Ray's Original Pizza® is a registered trademark of USA Famous Original Ray's Licensing Corp. SkyMall® is a registered trademark of SkyMall, Inc. Taser® is a registered trademark of TASER International, Inc. Tupperware® is a registered trademark of Tupperware Brands Corporation. Twister™ is a trademark of HASBRO. Velcro® is a registered trademark of Velcro Industries B. V. Velveeta® is a registered trademark of Kraft Foods Holdings, Inc. Viagra® is a registered trademark of Pfizer Inc. Virgin Atlantic® is a registered trademark of Virgin Atlantic Airways Limited. Walkman® is a registered trademark of Sony Corporation.